Table of Contents

A Word from the Author   1
    An Encouragement as You Begin

Chapter 1   Building Houses and Marriages   4
    A Life-Changing Talk with Grandpa

Chapter 2   Dreaming and Designing   15
    When Expectations and Reality Meet

Chapter 3   Following the Blueprint   31
    Wow! Talk About a Beautiful Plan

Chapter 4   Building upon a Great Foundation   46
    Anything Else is Absolutely Foolish

Chapter 5   Decorating and Furnishing   72
    Making Your Home Unique and Special

Chapter 6   Watching for Anything Harmful   99
    Big Storms, Bad Thieves, and Little Bugs

Chapter 7   Overcoming Procrastination   132
    Fix the Little Things Before They Become Big

Chapter 8   Enjoying the Seasons   157
    Keep Looking Forward to Eternity

Epilogue   So Now It Is Up To You   196
    What a Joy to be Married to your Best Friend

To my wife Karen who truly is my best friend.
The honeymoon is over, but the friendship isn't!
She is my encourager and the love of my life.

Thanks to Mrs. Becky Little and Mrs. Karen Peck for their work of proof reading the manuscript. Special thanks to Mrs. Ginny Sebok for the hours she has invested editing my writing. Her patience and diligence are so greatly appreciated.

bcpusa.org

The Journey of a Lifetime 3

Pardon the Dust!
Our Marriage is Under Construction

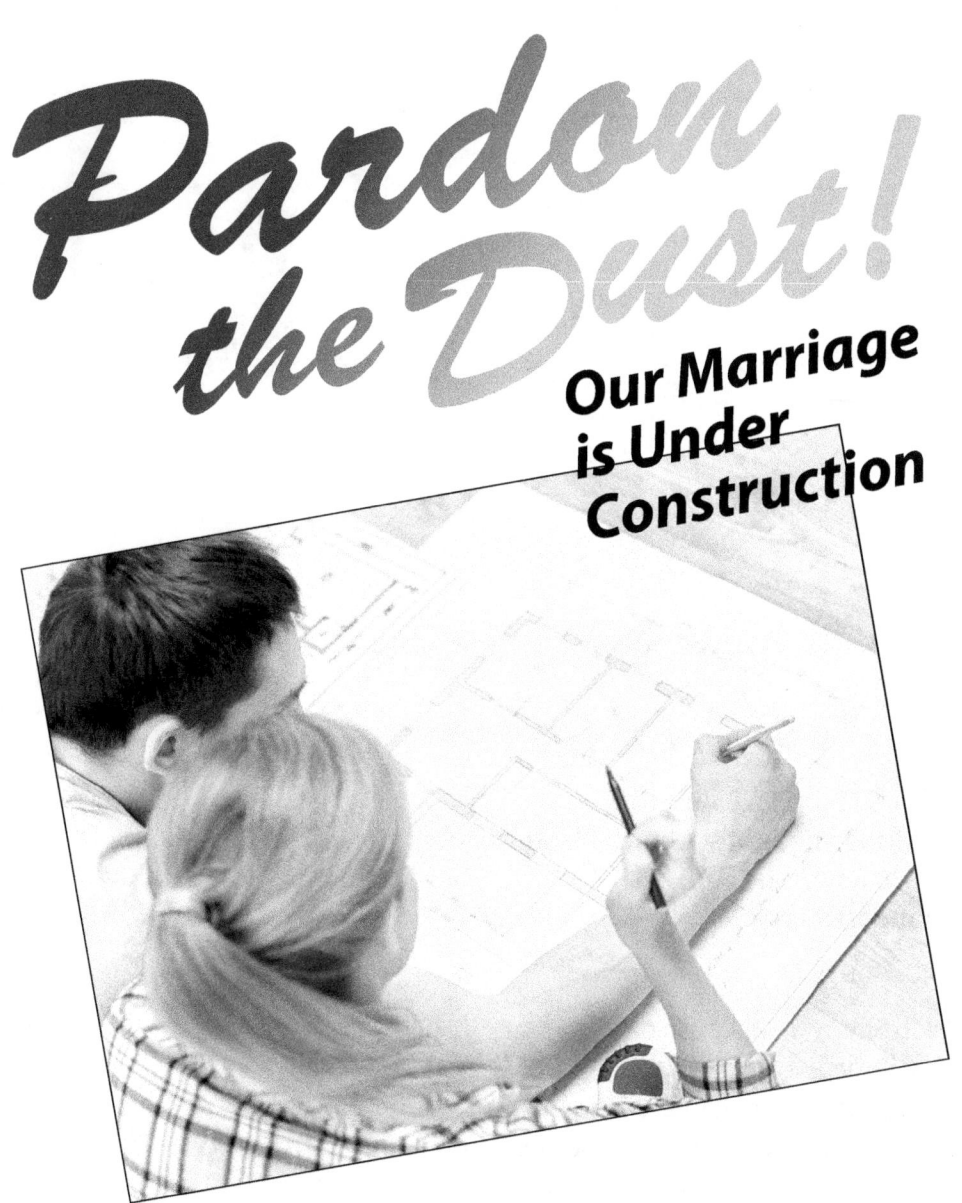

Dr. Michael J. Peck

Except where noted, Scripture quotations are from the Authorized King James Version of the Holy Bible. Scripture taken from the New King James Version® (NKJV) Copyright © 1982 by Thomas Nelson. Used by permission. All rights reserved.

ISBN 978-1-936285-05-1
Published by Baptist Church Planters
36830 Royalton Road
Grafton, Ohio 44044

440-748-1677

Web Site: www.bcpusa.org
Email: bcp@bcpusa.org
© Baptist Church Planters 2015
Book design by an idea—anideaweb.com

A Word from the Author

An Encouragement as You Begin

Everyone knows that some marriages are in trouble. Probably more couples are in trouble than some people realize. Think of the enemies that are set on harming or destroying marriages. Without question, the enemies of the home and family are numerous.

Satan, sin, selfishness, and stubbornness wreak havoc in the American home and family. Pornography is one such blight as it destroys the special bond of "we are reserved for each other." The number of couples who are living together without the commitment of marriage continues to grow. In many regions of our country, the rate of divorce hovers at nearly the fifty percent mark. Children are growing up in homes where fighting has become common place. Obviously, the state of marriage today is under attack.

That's the bad news. Here is good news! There is hope and help for any marriage. You may be thinking that it is too late and it is too hopeless for your marriage to change. I want to assure you that it is certainly not too late for you and your spouse. Please take a moment to read and think about the following references. These Absolutes provide the strong foundation upon which you may securely build.

God gave the directions, and the Word of God still works (Isaiah 55:11). This book that you are holding is saturated with Scripture and Scriptural principles that work! The Bible is God-breathed and is still able to accomplish what otherwise would be impossible. The Word of God is effective and powerful. Every married couple needs to get into the Scriptures. You need to develop a pattern of consistent reading and applying of God's Word. It will be amazing to see the Lord work in special ways.

The Holy Spirit possesses life-changing power (Romans 8:26-27). People cannot make other people change. You cannot make your spouse change, nor can your spouse change you! Perhaps you have experienced near desperation when the people you care about and deeply love are making unwise choices. You so much want your loved ones to know the blessing and joy that comes from dedicating their lives to the Lord. When they don't respond, you are saddened and even frustrated.

I know you have heard it many times before, but it is so true. Please remember that although you cannot make a person change, there is One that *can* bring about change in a person's life. It is the Holy Spirit Who takes the Word, brings conviction, and then enables individuals to make the changes they need to make. You will be wise if you do not try to play the part of the Holy Spirit in the life of your spouse, family, or even your friends. He alone can produce lasting change!

The Lord's incredible wisdom is available for the asking (James 1:5). It is wonderful to know that the wisdom of the Lord is personal, powerful, and practical. Best of all, it is available to couples as well as to individuals. It's yours for the asking! Go ahead. Ask Him for lots of wisdom. He has plenty to give, and He greatly desires to answer your prayer.

As you read this book and build a beautiful marriage, you will need wisdom in applying the principles of God's awesome Blueprint. You will need wisdom to understand yourself and your spouse. You will need wisdom as you begin the most wonderful building project in the entire world—your marriage!

Picture the foundation of a life built on Christ (Matthew 7:24-27). Wise believers still build their lives, marriages, and families upon the Lord and His Word. He is the Rock, the solid Foundation upon which it is safe and secure to build lives. The time that you are investing will be well worth the effort of going back to the starting point and rebuilding that which is wounded and damaged. He is the Rock. He is the awesome and sure Foundation. There is nothing comparable upon which you may wisely and safely build your life and marriage.

Demolishing is fast; building strong marriages takes time (Joshua 24:15; Luke 1:37). Sometimes the devastation seems insurmountable. You see the number of homes splitting up, marriages ending in divorce and couples who are still together but so very disconnected. This might seem pretty discouraging. If your marriage is encountering problems, you may be tempted to give up. Others have. They've quit. Why not you?

The good news is that there are hundreds of couples who are determined to find answers to the following questions.

- Why are we not close like we used to be?
- How did we end up where we are today?
- Why do we seem to be so distant from each other?
- In our early years together we were best friends? When did this stop?
- How do we return? How do we get back to where things used to be?
- How do we become best friends again?

It may look hopeless to some! Others may doubt that any change could take place. Sometimes this doubt is openly voiced. For others the wound is silent but very deep.

But an amazing thing for many couples begins to take place after asking such questions. Love can be rekindled. Sins can be confessed and couples turn from these. Forgiveness can be extended. Lives can slowly but surely change. Couples actually can become best friends again!

It is my great desire and earnest prayer that this book will bless you and your marriage. I guarantee that the construction will be well worth the effort. May you *become* best friends again, or even better, may you *stay* best friends even though the honeymoon's over! You are about to enter a precious construction as you build a Godly and beautiful marriage.

Michael J. Peck

Proverbs 3:5-6

Chapter One
Building Houses and Marriages

A Life-Changing Talk with Grandpa

"This is my beloved, and this is my friend, O daughters of Jerusalem" (Song of Solomon 5:16)

*Sometimes the greatest lessons
come to us from those who have walked ahead of us!
Take time to learn from older folks.
You might be surprised at their wisdom and humor.*

Tomorrow would be their eighteenth wedding anniversary. It didn't seem possible that these many years had passed by so quickly. After their children were in their beds for the night, Tim and Kirsten sat down for a time of reading the Bible and prayer together. They reminisced about their wedding ceremony rehearsal. They laughed about the best man pretending to faint. They remembered Grandpa Mitchell and thanked the Lord for his investment in their lives. It was he who had helped Tim begin the journey of "staying best friends long after the honeymoon was over."

Tim was now one of the partners in the family construction business. He often thought back to the day that Grandpa Mitchell had given him the list to which he had adhered as the founder of the business. Grandpa Mitchell had told him that the principles of building a beautiful house would be true for building a beautiful marriage.

After devotions were over and Kirsten went to make a phone call, Tim sat quietly on the couch and thought back to that visit with his Grandpa Mitchell a little over nineteen years ago. It would set the direction for

Tim's marriage, and he remembered it with great detail like it had happened yesterday.

Over nineteen years before this…

It was the first time that Timothy Mitchell had visited his grandparent's home since the announcement of his engagement to Kirsten O'Toole. Things were different on this visit. Tim had always loved going to Grandpa and Grandma's house, and this day was no different in his love for his grandparents. But things were very different this time for Tim.

Today Tim would visit as a twenty-four year old engaged man. He was filled with love for his beloved Kirsten, but he was also greatly shaken with the events of the past few days in his local church. Two key people in his church family, Anthony and Amy Madison, had announced to the shock of many that their lives had been miserable the last five or six years and that they were going to get a divorce.

"Not the Madisons!" Tim had thought when he heard the news. He was crushed. He couldn't believe it.

Many thoughts raced through the mind of this young fiancé. On one hand he grieved over the Madisons' announcement; on the other hand he was excited about his engagement. He looked forward to talking about all of this with his grandparents. He was scared that if divorce could happen to the Madisons, it surely could happen to Kirsten and him as well.

In spite of the fearful emotions that wildly raced through his mind, Tim quieted himself as he remembered that Pastor Ahrens would give them good advice in premarital counseling. They had already purchased their premarital materials "From This Time Forward—Preparing Couples for the Journey of a Lifetime," even though he and Kirsten had not yet started their program. But a nagging unsettledness kept gnawing away at him. What would his marriage be like?

Walking down the sidewalk at his grandparent's home always brought back great memories. Grandpa and Grandma Mitchell had lived in this beautiful ranch style home from the time Tim was a little baby. Many of his growing up childhood memories had taken place in this home.

The sun was shining through the large oak trees, providing a welcoming look. Warm splashes of delightful sunlight and shadows seemed to dance on the same sidewalk that Tim had played on many years ago. He thought about the joy and gladness that thrived in this house and said to himself, "Here is a beautiful home with two dear people that have a beautiful marriage. I want my marriage to be like theirs."

"Hello there, favorite grandson!" Grandpa called from the front porch, interrupting Tim's thoughts.

Tim laughed and called back, "Well, that's not too great of a compliment seeing that I am your only grandson." Laughing from that little joke, Tim quickly climbed the stairs and walked toward his grandfather. Slowly pushing himself up from the white wicker rocking chair, Grandpa took Tim into his arms.

"It's always good to see you, Tim," Grandpa said softly as he hugged his very tall grandson. "Grandma and I always love the times that you have been able to stop by after school. I've always considered it a privilege that your dad and mom live just a few blocks from here. I've watched you grow up, Tim, into the fine man that I'm mighty proud to call my grandson," the elderly Mark Mitchell said tenderly. With that he punched the shoulder of his one-and-only grandson!

Tim smiled and sat down on the other wicker porch chair, enjoying the wonderful late summer morning with his precious grandparents. Lunch would be ready soon, and the men would surely enjoy grandmother's cooking. She always assured Tim that she wasn't fussing. But the way she loved to cook for her grandson, home from college, would make you think that Tim had not had a good meal in over a month!

After a few moments of chatting, Grandpa turned to his grandson and said, "Tim, we are so happy about your engagement to Kirsten. I love her as if she were my own born granddaughter. You two are such a Godly and precious couple. Your grandma and I pray for you two every day, and we thank the Lord for you."

Tim thanked his grandpa but seemed to be kind of quiet today. It wasn't long before Grandpa sensed this and said, "You know, I have been your grandpa for a good number of years. It seems like I can always sense when something's bothering you, my precious grandson. Is everything all right, Tim?"

"You're right, Grandpa. I never have been able to hide anything from you. Don't get me wrong. I really am very excited about our engagement. And I really, really do love Kirsten. It's just..." Tim seemed to stutter and stumble for the right word. "Well, Grandpa, let me put it this way. I guess I'm just really afraid. With the word coming out about the Madisons.... well, Grandpa, with this kind of news coming so close to our engagement, it has me scared. The Madisons seemed to be the ideally married couple," Tim said as he turned to his grandfather.

"I know, Tim. We were all shocked to hear the announcement. Our hearts are broken for them. Guess I'd have to say that I'm even more heartsick for their children and their little granddaughter. It doesn't seem possible to any of us," Grandpa said quietly. Without realizing it, Tim and his grandpa actually began rocking in a synchronized motion. When they realized it, they both burst out laughing. That seemed to break the ice for Tim.

"Grandpa," Tim said, still laughing from their rocking rhythm, "I want my marriage to be like yours and Grandma's. You've been married over fifty years, and yet you and Grandma....well, let's just say....well, you guys just absolutely love each other!"

Grandpa burst out laughing and said, "Oh dear! You mean it shows?"

Tim laughed out loud and said, "Oh, Grandpa! Does it ever! Seriously, Grandpa, I am so shaken by the Madisons' divorce. Kirsten and I will begin our premarital counseling with Pastor Ahrens within the next couple of weeks, and by the time Pastor is finished, we will have met six or seven times. From what my friends have told me about the pastor's Biblical counseling program, he will talk to us about every situation of marriage, so that is good. Kirsten and I already have our books. The title is something about the Journey of a Lifetime. But Grandpa, let me just....well, may I ask you a question?"

Building Houses and Marriages 7

"Tim, I like to think that you have been able to talk to me about anything," Grandpa said earnestly. "Go ahead. I may not have the answer, but you feel free to ask anything you wish," Grandpa Mitchell assured Tim.

"Thanks, Grandpa. Here's the question. How did you and Grandma do it? What did you two do to arrive at such a successful marriage? When we reach your age, we want to have such a marriage as yours," Tim spoke quietly but with the force of genuine conviction.

Grandpa was silent for a moment. Tim looked up to discover tears streaming down Grandfather Mitchell's worn cheeks. Grandpa stopped rocking and shifted slightly in his rocking chair so that he could look squarely at his grandson. It was a moment that Timothy Mitchell would never forget. He expected a grand and lengthy answer. Grandpa Mitchell's answer was striking in its brevity. Grandpa often talked in lengthy sentences. This time he was very brief.

"We became best friends, and we stayed that way," Grandpa said. "That's it, Tim. We stayed best friends." Mark Mitchell took the handkerchief from his pocket to wipe his eyes. "It may sound funny, Tim, but I not only *love* your grandmother, I like her, too! She is my best friend!"

Neither said anything for a few moments. It was not until Grandmother Mitchell pushed open the screen door and said, "Why Timmy! I didn't know you were here already. Good thing I checked because lunch is just about ready. Now come on, you two. Wash up and come to the table, and let's eat. Tim, you must be starved, and I've made your favorite lunch. Hope you're hungry because I made a-plenty!" Evelyn Mitchell said as she brought the piping hot food to the already set table.

They enjoyed their lunch together reminiscing over happy experiences that Tim, his siblings, and their cousins had had at Grandpa and Grandma Mitchell's house while growing up. It was a wonderful lunch. The conversation around the table that day started Timothy on a journey with his Kirsten that would last a lifetime.

"Tell me more about staying best friends," Tim said to his Grandpa. "Just how did you and Grandma stay best friends? Surely there must have been hard times. I've never heard either of you speak harshly to each other, but certainly there must have been times when you disagreed. I know you both have very different personalities, and if I remember correctly, you came from very different backgrounds. Just exactly how did you become best friends and stay that way?" Tim prodded.

Grandpa Mitchell took one more swallow of his coffee, and placing the cup carefully upon the saucer, he thoughtfully looked up at his grandson and said, "It's just like building a house. Did you know our family business just finished house number 517? There are certain things that are true about every single one of those houses," Grandpa said, tapping his finger on the table for emphasis. "If you build your marriage the same way I build houses, well, at least like I used to, and the way the family business still does, you'll stay best friends," Grandpa said as he looked at his beloved Evelyn and winked at her.

Evelyn gazed back at her husband, smiled and turned to her grandson and said, "Timmy, a few years after we were married, we were both frightened to find out that neither one of us was happy in our marriage. We really were scared because we didn't even like each other. In that day-and-age divorce was not an option, but I can tell you that I absolutely could not imagine spending the rest of my life with this man. He was not the man that I had married," Grandma said seriously.

The Mitchells had decided ahead of time that if the subject should ever come up, they wanted to share with their only grandson the story of their journey in marriage. Now it was not a case of "if the subject comes up" as Tim had that very subject on his mind and heart. Both of his grandparents were happy to share with him about their lives and the great turnabout in their marriage.

"It hit me hard one night, Tim," Grandpa said, turning to his grandson, who by this time had stopped eating and was in a state of shock to hear that his grandparents at one time had both been unhappy in their marriage. "I mean, it hit me really hard! How was it that I could build beautiful homes, but I couldn't build a beautiful marriage? Then it dawned on me. The same principles that I would use to build a beautiful house would also build a lasting and beautiful marriage," Mark Mitchell said.

"Please, Grandpa, tell me exactly what those principles are. Even though you, my dad, and each of my uncles are in the construction business, I don't see what that has to do with building a lasting and happy marriage," Tim said with total seriousness. He nearly choked on the mashed potatoes as he contemplated that his dear grandparents at one time had been very unhappy in their marriage and didn't even like each other. He scarcely could believe it as he looked at them now. "What an amazing change took place in your lives!" he said.

"We'll write them down after lunch," Grandpa said to Tim. "But for now, let me just tell you that there are several things folks must do as they build their marriage. If couples will make a commitment to do the same things our company is committed to doing in building beautiful houses that last, they will become best friends. I guarantee it," Mark Mitchell said.

Grandpa Mitchell had begun the family business still called "Mitchell and Sons Construction." Mark and his four sons and their families love the Lord Jesus Christ. Soon after the family business was named, someone came up with the motto "We don't just build houses – we build homes!" The Mitchell and Sons Construction became widely known for the beautiful homes they built as well as the Godly principles by which they operated.

Tim and his grandparents always enjoyed their time together. Grandmother's lunch was delicious, and before long it was time for Tim to be going. Grandpa moved his plate away and wrote out the list that Mark would take with him. Mark never forgot that day.

"Tim, here are the things I always talk to couples about as they get ready to build their new home. If you and Kirsten will do the same things in your marriage, then you will be best friends even when the honeymoon's over. Here is what I tell folks who want a house.

> *Remember these seven things:*
>
> *First, you have to think about the design of it. What kind of house do you want?*
>
> *Second, you have to follow the architectural plans.*

Third, you need to build upon a good solid foundation.

Fourth, as the house is built, it stands empty and will echo, so you need to furnish it and decorate it.

Fifth, over the years you need to watch out for anything that will harm the structure of your house. I always tell folks around this part of the country that they need to keep their eyes open for tornadoes, thieves, and termites!

Sixth, you need to keep repairing things when they break down. I tell folks not to procrastinate. If something breaks, fix it right away when it is little!

Last, you just plain simply need to enjoy the seasons that will come as a homeowner.

This is how I build beautiful houses. This is the same formula that your grandmother and I used to build a beautiful marriage. Always remember how much your grandmother and I love you and Kirsten. Take no shortcuts. Seek the Lord daily. Build your marriage like I build houses. Grandpa"

Tim indeed cherished the seven things his grandfather had written out for him. With his very own eyes he had seen his beloved grandfather and now the rest of his family become the premier builders in their county. Even when other builders had no construction going on, Mitchell and Sons Construction had a waiting list of people wanting them to build their new houses. If these are the seven principles that made the family business so successful in building houses, and if Grandfather and Grandmother had committed themselves to the same principles when their marriage was unhappy, seeing the end result convinced Tim that he wanted to implement the same principles and staying best friends with Kirsten, not only now in their engagement, but throughout the years of their marriage.

Tim took the little card with Grandpa Mitchell's poor handwriting which summarized the seven things that build successful houses as well as marriages. Getting into his car after his precious visit and pulling onto the highway in front of his grandparent's home, he looked up to see his grandparents standing on the front porch. They waved goodbye with one hand and were holding hands with the other. Quietly Tim whispered to the Lord, "They stayed best friends. Lord, that is what I want for Kirsten and me. I want to stay best friends long after the honeymoon's over."

Later that afternoon when Kirsten finished her shift at work, Tim picked her up to go on their date for supper after which they went for a walk in the community park. An old park bench that apparently was forgotten by most folks in town had become a favorite spot to them. They loved to sit beside the little stream known as "Miller's Creek" and listen to the water gurgling as it flowed by.

"Honey," Tim said as he took her hand, "today was an incredible day. I know you are looking forward to our premarital counseling, and I am, too. But I've got to tell you, Sweetheart. I think today I found the real key to us having a great marriage." Pulling out the handwritten note, he gave it to Kirsten to read.

"It was like I was taking a college course on successful house and marriage-building by two very wise and expert professors! If we build our marriage the same way Grandpa and his sons build houses and the way they built their marriages, we will do well. If the Rapture doesn't come in our lifetime, fifty years from now, Kirsten, I want you to be my best friend even though our honeymoon will be long over!" Tim spoke tenderly.

"I couldn't ask for anything more than that, Honey," Kirsten said after reading the note. "With the Lord as the Head of our home and your grandpa's formula for building beautiful houses and marriages, I really believe we can stay best friends." As they hugged, she lovingly whispered, "I love you, Timothy Mark Mitchell!"

Over nineteen years later…

Kirsten returned from the phone call and asked Tim, "What are you so deep in thought about?"

Tim looked up and said, "Thinking about Grandpa Mitchell and his little note on building houses and building marriages." He got up from the couch and walked to the desk in their family room. "It's been a while since I read Grandpa's note. On the eve of our anniversary, it's a good time to pull it out and read it once more." It only took a moment to find that note written now over nineteen years ago.

Walking back to Kirsten with the note in his hand, he sat down beside her, and together they read that worn and wrinkled note.

"Tim, here are the things I always talk to couples about as they get ready to build their new home. If you and Kirsten will do the same things in your marriage, then you will be best friends even when the honeymoon's over. Here is what I tell folks who want a house.

Remember these seven things:

First, you must think about the design of it. What kind of house do you want?

Second, you have to follow the architectural plans.

Third, you need to build upon a good solid foundation.

Fourth, as the house is built, it stands empty and will echo, so you need to furnish it and decorate it.

Fifth, over the years you need to watch out for anything that will harm the structure of your house. I always tell folks around this part of the country that they need to keep their eyes open for tornadoes, thieves, and termites!

Sixth, you need to keep repairing things when they break down. I tell folks not to procrastinate. If something breaks, fix it right away when it is little!

Last, you just plain simply need to enjoy the seasons that will come as a homeowner.

This is how I build beautiful houses. This is the same formula that your grandmother and I used to build a beautiful marriage. Always remember how much your grandmother and I love you and Kirsten. Take no shortcuts. Seek the Lord daily. Build your marriage like I build houses. Grandpa"

Building Houses and Marriages 13

It had been a while since Tim and Kirsten had read Grandpa's note. Though he had since gone home to be with the Lord, Grandpa's investment in Tim and Kirsten's marriage continued to be such a blessing.

"I'm so glad you visited your grandparents that day," Kirsten said as she took his hand. "With the Lord's help, we have done these things over the years, and Sweetheart, you really are my best friend," she lovingly said. "Your grandpa was so right," she quietly said.

"How absolutely blessed I am," Tim responded. "It surely hasn't been perfect. We've both made our fair share of mistakes, but just as Grandpa promised, good houses and good marriages are built upon the same principles," Tim continued.

"The honeymoon's long over, but here we are staying best friends!" Kirsten said with a smile as she snuggled closer to her husband.

The time together continued throughout the next hour. Tim mentioned to his wife that their young friends Ken and Alisha would be meeting with his uncle. "Seems they think they're ready for Mitchell and Sons to build them a house," Tim said. Holding the time-wrinkled note his Grandfather Mitchell had written nineteen years earlier, he said, "It will be fun for us to watch Ken and Alisha walking though the Mitchell steps for beautiful houses. Maybe we ought to have them over for a meal and share these principles with them. I hope they will do the same things in their marriage."

Think about these questions

1. How would you define the word "friend"?

2. What do you think are some of the main characteristics of friendship?

3. Read Proverbs 24:3-4. What does this mean to you?

4. Based on your experience, what two or three key things would you suggest to help a newly engaged couple prepare for marriage?

5. In what ways did you implement the two or three things that you suggested for the newly engaged couple?

Chapter Two
Dreaming and Designing

When Expectations and Reality Meet

"...The LORD hath been witness between thee and the wife
of thy youth, against whom thou hast dealt treacherously:
yet is she thy companion, and the wife
of thy covenant" (Malachi 2:14)

Think about your expectations.
Do you think that they are realistic?
How do your expectations compare with the Scriptures?
Did you know that the Scriptures provide very clear teaching about the two
expectations of companionship based on this special covenant?
Did you know that you and your spouse should bring
these to your marriage?

From Grandpa's note: Think about the design. What are you expecting?

Key thought: *Keep in mind this simple definition of an expectation: <u>an expectation is what you think or anticipate that a person, place, or thing will be.</u> Everyone has expectations about people or situations. Sometimes the expectations are not very well thought through.*

Malachi spoke to the husbands of his day who obviously did not have reasonable expectations of their marriages. He addressed the situation with a not-so-very-happy message. In plain, simple words he pointed to treacherous husbands who were treating their wives with hurtful, disloyal, and wicked actions. Wives were being crushed emotionally by being divorced at the whim of their self-centered husbands.

It is a sad thing still today to witness a disloyal spouse who deliberately wounds the marriage partner. Sometimes the hurt comes through bitter words and unkind actions. The Lord God is saddened, family members are wounded, and ultimately, marriages are destroyed by such actions.

What would cause a spouse to become disloyal and begin to deal treacherously in the home? While there may be a number of contributing factors, perhaps one of the greatest reasons for such a situation is unmet expectations. Unreasonable and unfulfilled expectations result in great disappointments and often lead to divorce or at least treacherous actions that wound the marriage partner.

Think of this obvious and simple truth. Houses do not just build themselves; neither do successful and happy marriages. That may be so profoundly simple and obvious that most couples do not consider the importance of this statement. Houses and marriages both must start at the dreaming and designing stage. When building a house, the couple must meet with the general contractor in the planning stage. When building a marriage, wise couples must search the Scriptures and speak tenderly to each other about their dreams and expectations for their marriage.

Many couples never consider God's design for their marriage and home. Fewer and fewer couples seem to have the attitude of "Let's search the Scriptures to learn the ways of a Godly marriage." Was there ever a time that you and your spouse sat together and actually formulated a list of the expectations each had for the other, for self, and for the marriage? Have you together considered and written out a list of what the Lord desires for your marriage?

Dreams and Designs for Houses

The day came for Ken and Alisha to sit down across the desk of the builder, Henry Mitchell. They came in with fears as well as much excitement. They were ready to talk about their "dream home." Henry Mitchell smiled. Here was another couple with big expectations that probably were not realistic.

"It's amazing how many kinds of houses are available," Henry Mitchell said. "One site in my builder's manual lists over seventy-five styles of homes. These homes are as different from each other as you can imagine. There are American Colonial, the Bungalow, the Cape Cod, the rustic Log Home plan, the sprawling Ranch style, and the ornate Victorian, as well as dozens of other home styles."

"We made a list of the things that we think we want," Alisha mentioned as she pulled the list from her purse.

"Well, that's great," Henry said. "Let's see what your expectations are for dreaming and designing your house." He reached across his desk and took the list.

"One of the first things that I as the builder will work through with you is to determine if your budget matches your dreams. You might have the dream house in your minds, but perhaps you do not have your dream bank account to match it," Henry Mitchell said with a half-smile. "Now let's take a look at what you have written down for me to see. What are your expectations and dreams for your new house?"

Ken and Alisha had big expectations. Ken's dad had tried to warn Ken that his expectations were not completely realistic. Ken and Alisha had drawn a sketch of a house that was just under 4,000 square feet, complete with five bedrooms, four bathrooms, and an open concept kitchen with a large formal dining area. Just off their very large master bedroom was a large bathroom with a Jacuzzi. Ken wanted a large family room, and Alisha wanted a full kitchen area at the end of the family room to make snacks for their guests. In the front they wanted a beautiful porch, and in the back of the house they drew a multi-level deck. Of course they wanted their home to be located in a beautiful park-like setting.

"Well," Ken asked, "what do you think of our expectations?"

Here comes the big crash. Ken and Alisha's expectations and reality collide.

Dreaming and Designing

Henry Mitchell looked at the list, and then looked at them. Returning to the list, he started figuring and calculating. Reality was about to strike!

"Well, Ken and Alisha, here is a rough idea of what your expectations are going to cost. Right now, if we were to buy the land and build the house that you have sketched out, I would say conservatively speaking that we would be right around $600,000, probably a little more," Henry Mitchell said as he pushed the calculator away.

Stunned, Ken looked at Alisha in a state of disbelief. "You are kidding, aren't you, Mr. Mitchell?" Ken said as he glanced back at the smiling contractor. "This isn't what we expected at all. How much of a house can you build us for closer to $175,000?"

Henry Mitchell pulled from his shelves an attractive and professional notebook of the homes in various price categories that his company could build. "In your price range we have to downsize your expectations because of your budgetary reality," Henry said as he opened the notebook. "I would say we could build you a very nice 1,700 square feet house with three bedrooms, 1½ bathrooms, and a nice kitchen. However, it will be about half the size you were hoping for. You can have a pleasant dining room but no family room, or we can build a family room but no dining room, whichever you choose. And I must tell you that your house will not be located in a park-like setting. Your dreams and expectations are just not realistic. I'm sorry, folks," Henry Mitchell said to the disappointed couple.

Expectations and reality were far apart! Sometimes the same thing is true in marriage. Sometimes expectations are not realized because they are unrealistic and unreasonable.

Dreams and Designs for Marriage

Beautiful marriages, like beautiful houses, do not just happen. So let's stop right here and ask the question, "What were you expecting that your marriage would be like at this point in your lives?"

Most things begin with dreaming and designing. The same will be true for you and your spouse, if you want to either become best friends or stay best friends in your marriage. You really do need to talk about realistic expectations with your spouse in the dreaming and designing of your marriage. Remember that these expectations are not a list of harsh demands; rather, they are the hopes and the dreams that you have about your marriage. This happens by investing time to talk, share, laugh together, study the Bible together and individually, asking questions that will clarify what your spouse is saying, and praying together about what God's expectations are for your marriage.

So honestly, what are your expectations?

Sadly, you may have spent more time talking about your weeklong vacation than about your marriage. You and your spouse may have unspoken expectations of what you want your marriage to look like. Unfortunately, because these expectations may never have been discussed, you may be assuming that your spouse automatically knows what you are thinking. If your expectations are not reasonable, you may even be experiencing resentment because of these unfulfilled expectations. To stay best friends, wise couples will invest very special time talking about their dreams or expectations.

Remember this definition: an expectation is what you think or anticipate that a person, place, or thing will be.

The key words are "what you think" it should be. Problems arise in marriage when expectations are not fulfilled.

Unreasonable expectations coming from husbands that lead to a crash

- He expects that his wife will do things just the way his mother did.
- He expects that when he comes home tired from work that she will always take care of the parenting, at least most of it, so that he can relax.
- He expects that she will keep the house like his mother did, which means that she will pick up after him (even if he doesn't put it into those exact words).
- He expects that somehow she will always be ready for intimacy at nearly a moment's notice. It is half-time in the football game they are watching in the family room. With a silly grin he says, "We have twenty minutes. Are you in the mood?" Typically the answer will be

"NO!" He forgets that his wife does not think the same way he does. This is especially true with intimacy.
- He expects that she will deeply respect him. He expects that she will admire him and tell him often how proud she is of his work. He expects to be appreciated for his efforts and respected because of what he does and the positon he holds, even if he doesn't always live up to his own standards.
- He expects that she will know what he is thinking because probably he will be a man of very few words.
- Oh yes, and did we mention intimacy? Even though he is too tired to talk throughout the evening (which his wife really desires), and often he is too tired to help with the children, quite often he later revives to the point that he expects that she will have enough energy for intimacy before they go to sleep for the night.

Do you really think that any of these expectations are remotely realistic? Of course not. Somehow when you read them in print they really stand out in their elevated state of "you've got to be kidding me." If you are the husband, have you ever entertained any of these expectations?

Unreasonable expectations coming from wives that lead to a crash

- She expects that her husband will consistently love and cherish her just like she reads in the Bible that "Christ loves the Church and gave Himself for it." That, of course, is not the problem. Husbands should indeed love their wives the way that Christ loves the Church. The problem comes in how the wife expects that this Christ-like love will be demonstrated.
- She expects that her husband will be good at being affectionate and romantic. "If he can fix broken pipes and trim unwanted tree branches, then he can surely care for me," she thinks. She expects that if he really loves her he will be good at being romantic and expressing his love in tender words.
- She expects that her husband will hold her hand upon getting home from work and will be eager to listen to all the details of her day. She expects that his attention will be nearly fixated upon her as she relates how her day has gone, who she met at the store, as well as the dozen

other things she wants to tell him. She expects that his attention and interest will remain focused as she talks and shares with him.
- She expects that intimacy will begin in the kitchen as her husband helps with the dishes, speaks romantically to her of intimate things throughout the evening, and assures her that he finds her attractive and exciting. This will be nurtured throughout the evening as he helps with the children, and they slowly and romantically proceed toward the bedroom over the three or four hour period of intentional "preparation" time.
- She expects that her husband will be thoughtful, talkative and willing to share the details of his day, and will find many different ways to communicate to her that she is cherished.
- She expects that her husband will sense what she is thinking. It may be a total surprise for her to discover that her husband does not think the same way she thinks and often has no clue as to how she arrived at a particular point in a discussion.
- She expects that her husband will do things the way her father did things. If her father was a great role model, she might have unrealistic expectations that her husband will have the same level of maturity at twenty-five as her father had at fifty-five! This can be a really huge expectation that often is not met.

You may have smiled or even laughed out loud because these expectations are so unreasonable. If you are the wife, have you ever entertained any of these expectations?

Unbelievable expectations from both husband and wives and big reality crashes

Serving couples in premarital counseling is a true blessing and great responsibility as well. Some couples have very realistic expectations relating to marriage, home, and family; however, it is not uncommon to discover a couple that is very immature and whose expectations are not only unreasonable, they actually are almost humorous. These are some of the immature and unreasonable expectations actually heard in the counseling center:

- I will change my spouse after we are married.
- Marriage can't be all that hard. It will all just come naturally.

- My spouse will always appreciate me.
- Being in debt isn't so bad. Everybody else I know is as well.
- We'll always agree on the decisions we face. That won't be difficult.
- Parenting won't be so bad. I don't think it will change our lives all that much.
- Intimacy will always be as enjoyable as we have read about it being. It will just come automatically, and we will both enjoy it. I'm sure we will both view it the same way.
- It will be easy to follow the Lord.
- Our house will always be neat and orderly; everything will be arranged and ready if company should drop by.
- My husband will automatically be the spiritual leader of the home.
- My wife will always respect me and will submit as the Church submits to the Lord Jesus.

When you really stop and think about the matter of "expectations," there are bits and pieces of truth in many of these statements. Our homes ought not to be cluttered, dirty, and overrun with cobwebs. Sometimes spontaneity in intimacy is deeply rewarding. Arriving home to a good hot meal that is nearly ready is a wonderful blessing. Helping with the household chores and listening to each other is wonderful. There's nothing necessarily *wrong* in any of these areas; it's just that some of them are *unrealistic*. Read the list again and spot what is unreasonable.

It really struck the pastor that Sunday morning. He had prepared a practical message on the home and family. It had been a wonderful time for the pastor as he studied, prayed, wrote, and prayed some more! Just before the message, the choir sang a beautiful hymn about the home; suddenly it deeply touched his heart. Here's what really struck him. As he looked out over his congregation, there were many--nearly twenty-five-- married couples seated in the congregation, listening to the beautiful words celebrating the Lord's gracious goodness in their homes. He was struck by the great diversity within the marriages of his church family!

Several of the couples had been married for less than a year. Quickly he started to calculate how many had been married for five years, ten years, and twenty-five years, and then he noticed the dear couple seated on the far side of the auditorium who that year had celebrated their sixty-second anniversary. What great diversity indeed!

Then he thought back over some of the counseling sessions he had had with several of these couples. As the choir continued singing, he thought about the book he had read earlier in the week which noted the 'failed expectations' which typically surface at specific stages of marriage. How true this seemed to be in his church family.

Sometimes the unreasonable expectations and crashes are almost predictable

Even though a marriage fracture can occur at any period throughout the lifetime journey, there seems to be three periods of time through which marriages are especially prone to the problem of failed expectations.

Within the first five to seven years

Some couples experience the "this is not what I signed up for" reality around the five to seven year mark of their marriage. You might be at this mile marker. Is this where you are in your marriage? Has this thought ever crossed your mind? Has it crossed your mind more than once?

You may have entered marriage with the unrealistic expectation that your marriage was going to be a lifelong honeymoon where everything works automatically and smoothly with little effort. Long before the five-year mark, you may have discovered that marriage is not quite what you had expected. Though you are just starting your marriage journey, things might even seem hopeless to you. Do any of these sound familiar?

- You never dreamed that your spouse would annoy you so much over such little things!
- You never expected that your spouse would misunderstand your motives and desires.
- You never thought that your spouse would be so different after the wedding. You thought you really knew your spouse before you were married, but there were so many things that surprised you about your spouse once you were married. Of course you may not exactly be the person your spouse thought you to be as well. Maybe there were a few surprises for your spouse!
- You never thought it would be so hard to conceive and have a baby, or on the other hand the opposite may be true. You never thought it

would be this easy to conceive, and to your amazement another baby is on the way already!

- You never thought it would really cost this much for living expenses, even though the pastor who was doing your premarital counseling forewarned you.
- You are amazed how easy it is to upset your spouse. It's almost like your spouse doesn't know and understand you.

Do any of these failed expectations cause a disconnection between you and your spouse? Do any of these describe your situation?

Around the fifteenth year of marriage

The second phase of potential disconnection because of failed expectations hits around this fifteen year period of marriage. Here you are. You have been married over a dozen years. Everyone thinks you have the model marriage, but in your heart you may be wrestling with specifically failed expectations that confront you daily. Among some of these typical failed expectations during this period include things which in reality are actually blessings. They just are not quite what you had expected.

- Children have been born. They are wonderful blessings; however, they certainly do add to the schedule in very demanding ways! Sleepless nights with a colicky baby, doctors' visits, dental visits, church and youth group activities, school functions, and a growing financial responsibility frequently add strain to the marriage.
- The unrealistic expectation of wanting to have the perfect family, with nearly perfect children, who nearly always are healthy and, of course, obedient and very compliant. This has long since evaporated as unrealistic expectations have all been replaced with that uncomfortable dose of reality.
- The toddler who kicks her little feet and defiantly looks at you as she screams, "No!" brought a reality check into your marriage. The report from school that your son was acting inappropriately has brought another sudden reality check. Then that moment when you and your wife were ready for intimacy and the knock came on your door and your beloved child said, "Mommy, I'm thirsty," really brought a sudden and dramatic reality check.

You never expected this to happen, and suddenly you wanted to scream, "Well, go and get a drink of water, and do not knock on my door for another twenty years!" Of course that would bring an unpleasant thought to your child's mind as well as make an interesting point of discussion the next day in school!

- Careers are becoming more and more challenging with greater demands. An opportunity or two for promotion has come. With it comes more hours and greater responsibilities. You never expected that work would be so hard and demanding! You didn't expect to come home so tired.

- You didn't expect that married life would be this busy between church, family, and work. Sometimes it may seem to you that there simply are not enough hours in the week.

Do any of these failed expectations cause a disconnection between you and your spouse? Do any of these describe your situation?

Between twenty-five to thirty-five years of marriage

By this stage you might be expecting that couples are safe from major problems or disconnecting. Not so, actually. Believe it or not, some couples in this stage may face very serious potential for disconnection. You and your spouse may have failed expectations which have been ignored for years because of the busyness of your lives and the hectic schedule you have managed. It is entirely possible that you and your spouse have not had a serious talk in months or even longer, do not share conversation, and seldom read the Word of God. As difficult as it is to admit, does this describe you in this stage of the marriage journey? Here are a few of the failed expectations of this period that you may be experiencing.

- You and your spouse have poured nearly every ounce of energy, time, and even finances into your children. Very little time and investment has taken place in your marriage because you have been so busy with church, school, and dozens of other activities. Now your children have left home. It's the empty nest era. Just when you think that it's going to be wonderful to be "just us," the harsh reality strikes. It is so apparent that you have invested little or no time or energy in your marriage, and now you two are strangers. You expected that it would be fun to be "just us," but here you are home alone with your spouse, and you do not know each other. In fact, you are no longer sure that you even like this stranger!

- You didn't know how hard it would be to think of what to talk about.
- You don't even know what your spouse enjoys. You have been so busy with your children that you suddenly realize that you are emotionally disconnected from your spouse. It feels like you hardly know much about your spouse today.
- You expected that the empty nest would be an absolutely wonderful era in your life. Now it has become a great disappointment because you are so very disconnected.
- Do you remember the Madisons way back in the early chapter of this book? That is exactly what had happened to them. They still had several children at home. They were busy. They always did things together as a family. They were always in a hurry trying to keep up with things. They sat together in church and smiled at people, but they were not investing in their marriage. Their expectations were not realized. They were disconnected. They became just housemates; they were no longer friends.

Do any of these failed expectations cause a disconnection between you and your spouse? Do any of these describe your situation?

What's reasonable when it comes to expectations and reality

Wise couples who really love the Lord need to be very realistic in their expectations. Two very reasonable expectations focus upon the idea of *covenant* and *companionship*. When couples view marriage as a covenant, a blessed companionship blossoms. What a unique connection! The Lord will fashion your union, and there will be such joy as you and your spouse grow closer to the Lord and to each other. This is the connection that creates best friendships. This is where reasonable and realistic expectations originate. We'll think more of these two words a little later.

We have invested much time and space in exposing unrealistic expectations. This is important because these unrealistic expectations cause deep wounds and horrible scars. The following expectations are reasonable because they are Biblical. These are realistic expectations for couples during every phase of marriage.

- We will trust the Lord Jesus Christ and look to Him for His blessings. We will invest time together reading God's Word and praying together as a couple.
- We will learn to adjust to each other's personalities, strengths, and weaknesses.
- We will resolve that changing our spouse is not our personal responsibility. Only the Lord can change our spouse. We commit to asking the Lord to change our selves as well.
- We will be kind and encouraging in our words. When we disagree about something, we will express our opinions and preferences carefully and wisely. We understand that words can bring about lasting hurts and wounds that will damage our marriage.
- We will be affectionate with each other. We will demonstrate our love not only by our words but by our actions as well.
- We will hold our marriage in high regard and guard against anything that could wound or damage it. We will be careful not to allow too many good things in our schedules nor too much busyness that will keep us from investing in our marriage. In spite of the many demands, we as a husband and wife will intentionally make time for each other. We will talk with each other and enjoy our very special relationship.

The Biblical basis for Godly expectations

Whether you are working on this in a small group or as a couple, take some time to talk and pray about how expectations are affecting your marriage.

Unreasonable expectations are dangerous. Dear couples experience pain, hurt, and disappointment when unrealistic expectations are met with reality. Unnecessary hurts and disappointments are so painful.

Reasonable Biblical expectations do not create unnecessary wounds and hurts. They are based upon the concepts introduced a little earlier. This concept is the covenant which produces companionship. These expectations are found in Malachi 2:14, "Yet is she thy companion, and the wife of thy covenant."

Two key words to always remember
Malachi shares two key words that good marriages exemplify and practice. The first is the word "covenant," and the second is "companion." While there will be other reasonable expectations in marriages, these are the foundational, the very core expectations, that both you and your spouse should expect. Upon these special expectations every other reasonable expectation can be built.

The key word "covenant"
The prophet Malachi selected the word "covenant," which is the Hebrew word *beriyth* (ber-EETH), meaning "the pledging of one's life." Marriage is not a contract. Think of it. A contract is specifically written with the intention that both parties must fulfill the demands of the agreement. If one party fails to fulfill the demands agreed upon, the other party is no longer obligated to the terms of the contract.

Marriage is so very different from that! Marriage is a covenant. This means that the husband and wife pledge their lives to each other. Ownership of your life is lovingly and intentionally given to another--your beloved. Think of the depths and beauty of this incredible covenant. It is the deliberate decision to give yourself to another. This does not mean that a wife allows herself to be trampled underfoot by an irresponsible and arrogant husband. Obviously she must be kept safe. This does not mean that the husband lives in danger because of the threats of a violent wife. Obviously he must be kept safe as well.

This concept of marriage being a covenant is a thing of beauty and devotion. It is reasonable to have the expectation that you and your spouse will view your marriage as a covenant. This is not a light matter; rather, it requires prayer, intentional devotion, careful attention, and lots of nurturing along the marriage journey of a lifetime!

The second keyword "companion"
The Hebrew word is *chabereth* (khab-EH-reth), which means "being united, to be in close fellowship, and association." It is the opposite of living in

cold, distant hostility. Rather than living with walls that separate you and your spouse, companionship is strengthened by the building of bridges. The companionship aspect of marriage is the thrust of this book. There is nothing as wonderful as being best friends with your mate after many years of marriage. The joy of being best friends is an incredible connection in Godly marriages. Staying best friends with your mate long after the honeymoon's over is much more than just a subtitle. It is the expectation of successful marriages.

Think of it! Two reasonable expectations for every marriage flow from the aspects of covenant and companionship. These are not things to be demanded. They are, however, to be expected, prayed for, encouraged, and nurtured throughout the lifetime of your marriage.

Think about these questions

Set a convenient time that works for you both. Hold hands and snuggle a little. Ask the Lord to bless your time together. Talk about these questions. Be honest with each other as well as be loving and gracious. Make the most of these moments.

1. Before you were married, what were several expectations that you and your spouse entertained? Can you remember any? Think hard!

2. At this stage of your lives, how would you and your spouse answer these questions?
   - What are your present expectations for your marriage?
   - What place does the Lord really have in your personal life and marriage?
   - What place does Scripture reading, prayer, church attendance, tithing, and serving have in your marriage expectations? Are you and your spouse in agreement about the importance of these things?
   - What is the condition of your marriage? Be gracious, but be honest.
   - Do you and your spouse agree on your parenting?
   - Are there things that are left unresolved because you and your spouse do not agree with each other? For instance, are you and your spouse in agreement over practical matters such as indebtedness, spending, how you spend your leisure time, and vacationing?

No marriage is going to be perfect; however, Godly couples wisely work on reasonable expectations. We should expect that because the Lord is the head of our homes we will seek to honor Him and love Him as the Lord of our lives. In our marriages, we expect that the covenant and companionship aspects will cause our friendship to become greater and greater. "If you know these things, happy are you if you do them" (John 13:17).

It is my prayer that there will be a little "dust" which is the evidence that you are working in this area in your marriage. Constructing a beautiful marriage is a lot like constructing a beautiful house!

Chapter Three
Following the Blueprint

Wow! Talk About a Beautiful Plan

"All Scripture is given by inspiration of God, and is profitable for doctrine, for reproof, for correction, for instruction in righteousness. That the man of God may be perfect, thoroughly furnished unto all good works"
(2 Timothy 3:16-17)

How awesome to know that our great God has spoken.
How incredible to understand that God wants to speak to you!
Come every day with the joyful anticipation of hearing from the awesome Architect.
Come alone to meet with your Lord.
Come together as a couple to worship Him.
He wants to make something very beautiful of your life and marriage.
He can accomplish this because He is the Designer of the Master Blueprint!

From Grandpa's note: Follow the plans. When you don't, you will be in trouble quickly.

Key thought: *A blueprint provides detailed plans to build your house. The Bible is your spiritual, eternal Blueprint. It shows you not only how to know the Lord, but how to build a great marriage, how to become best friends with your spouse, and how to be blessed in your life.*

There are situations that are mediocre and situations that are great. There are mediocre doctors and there are great doctors, mediocre pastors and great pastors, mediocre businesses and great businesses. Likewise, there are mediocre marriages, and there are great marriages. Which do you really want for your marriage? Mediocre or great?

The answer to moving from a mediocre marriage to a great marriage goes back to the matter of following the Blueprint. Some people are downright notorious for not reading and following directions. You would be wise never to hire someone to work with your plumbing or electrical who refuses to follow the directions. Directions are critical. Contractors know these directions as the master blueprints. In this chapter we will focus upon the importance of you and your spouse following God's Master Blueprint.

Ken and Alisha were so excited about the soon-to-begin construction of their new house. Following their wedding ceremony, they lived for several years in a very modest apartment. Saving as much as they possibly could, they realized that this would be the time for them to build their new house. With nervousness as well as excitement, they met with the contractor. After a thorough question-and-answer period of time, and with full explanations of what they could afford, Henry Mitchell of Mitchell and Sons Construction explained to them the steps they would have to take now that their expectations were reasonable.

During the course of that meeting he shared that they employed people who would work together in producing a blueprint. The first would be the architect who would be very concerned about designing the house to meet their needs and wishes. Henry explained to them that their architect had great experience and that she brought unique insights to the design.

The second person that would be very involved in working on the blueprint would be the engineer. The engineers in the Mitchell firm worked very closely with the architects. They ensured that the design would be safe and meet all of the codes. They would be meticulous in designing the blueprints.

Henry explained that he and his company would work very closely with their architect and would follow the blueprints to every minute detail.

With his company there would be no scrimping, saving, or shabby work to cut costs. The only way they could guarantee a safe, beautiful, and enjoyable house would be to follow the blueprint.

At the end of the meeting he looked the young couple in the eye and said, "Ken and Alisha, I tell all the people who want to hire us the same thing. My dad, brothers and I follow the Bible as our Blueprint. You can trust us with the building of your house. We take the Blueprint of the Scriptures for our life and service to you as well as the blueprint of our architectural and engineering department to design a safe and beautiful house for you. We build the house. You will get to build the home. Building a home goes much better if you both place your trust in the Lord Jesus Christ and invite Him to be the priority in your home and family. The Bible will be your Master Blueprint to follow."

Follow God's Blueprint

Doesn't sound so hard, does it? Well, it is not as easy as it sounds, but it will be so worth the time and effort to do what God says. While no marriage will ever be perfect, it is wonderful to know that God actually does have a Blueprint for us. As you are working on building genuine friendship in your marriage, it will be absolutely essential to follow the Blueprint. Imagine what would happen if the contractor looked at the blueprint and decided that he or she did not want to follow it. Disaster would strike sooner than later.

Blueprints provide the design for living as well as prevention from disaster by ensuring safety. How incredible it is to realize that the true and the living God, the creator of the universe, decided to write a letter to us, a Master Blueprint for life. This precious letter, the Scriptures, is the only book that our great God wrote. From our perspective we would say that He was not in a hurry to complete his manuscript. The Lord took over 1500 years and used forty different authors to write His letter, His Master Blueprint, to you.

As you are seeking to build friendship into your marriage, you must settle the matter in your heart that God's Blueprint is absolutely the final authority for life. The Apostle Paul would soon be going home to be with the Lord, and he greatly desired that his beloved Timothy would be fully equipped for the ministry ahead of him. So Paul told him something that may be amongst the very last things that Paul would tell his son in the faith. He writes of the origin of God's Word.

The Blueprint is inspired

Paul reminds Timothy that God's Blueprint, the Scriptures, is given by inspiration (2 Timothy 3:16a). The combination word that Paul employed for "inspiration" is *Theopneustos*. How powerful this is! *Theos* means "God." *Pneo* is the word "to breathe." This tells us that God's Word was breathed out from God.

The Apostle Peter also helps us to understand the grand and unique origin of the Scriptures. He writes, "For the prophecy came not in the old time by the will of man: but holy men of God spoke as they were moved by the Holy Spirit" (2 Peter 1:21). This being "moved" is the word *phero*, "to be borne along," which gives the idea of the wind filling the sail and the boat being borne along on the body of the water.

Even the best blueprints designed by the most dedicated and talented architects are not perfect. How different is God's Blueprint! The Word of God was given by the Lord Himself who breathed it out and into the holy writers who were supernaturally guided and borne along. No other book was composed in this manner. The Bible is God's Blueprint for every area of life, including marriage!

The Blueprint is reliable

Even if you don't need to be convinced, think again of the powerful description of the reliability of the Word of God. The Scriptures you hold in your hands are totally reliable and worthy of your trust and confidence.

- *It is pure.* "The Statutes of the LORD are right, rejoicing the heart: the commandments of the LORD is pure, enlightening the eyes" (Psalm 19:8).
- *It is trustworthy.* "All His Commandments are sure. They stand fast for ever and ever, and are done in truth and uprightness" (Psalm 111:7-8).

- ***It is true.*** "Thou art near, O LORD, and all Thy Commandments are truth" (Psalm 119:151).
- ***It is enduring.*** "The grass withereth, the flower fadeth: but the Word of our God shall stand for ever" (Isaiah 40:8).
- ***It is living and active.*** "For the Word of God is quick, and powerful, and sharper than any two-edged sword, piercing even to the dividing asunder of soul and spirit, and of the joints and marrow, and is a discerner of the thoughts and intents of the heart (Hebrews 4:12).

The Blueprint is profitable

Paul assured Timothy that the Word of God is inspired; therefore God's Word is profitable (2 Timothy 3:16b). Paul was moved of the Lord to select the word "profitable," which is *ophelimos*, meaning "to be useful." This speaks of the Scriptures being not only essential, helpful, and beneficial; the Scriptures are also useful. God's Word is practical when applied to everyday living. This includes marriage throughout every season.

God's Word is practical and useful for the newlywed as well as for those who have walked together for many decades. Read it. Trust it. Apply it. You will be amazed at the difference the Word of God makes.

How many times in a typical week do you read God's Word, the Bible?

How many times in a typical week do you read the Bible together as husband and wife?

Can you name two or three ways that the Bible has been used to direct your lives as a couple?

Enjoying the principles of God's Word in two very special places

We live in a land of many Bibles in our homes, but less and less Bible in our hearts. Our schedules are becoming busier and busier. Very honestly, you may be spending less and less time with your spouse. You may be feeling the pressure of a busy schedule and having less time for important things. Think about this. There are two extremely important daily times to help marriages become great. These are the supper table and the family worship time. Eating and worshipping together are perhaps the most significant times of the day for you as a married couple.

Your supper table. This ought to be a place of fellowship and enjoyable sharing. It should be a place of encouragement and laughter. There will be opportunities for the principles of the Lord to be implanted in your children at the supper table (Deuteronomy 6:6-8). The supper table gives you, as well as your family, the place to reconnect after the day away from each other. It provides the opportunity for sharing, enjoying each other, and for great conversation. Even if it is just you and your spouse at the supper table, it is such an important time for conversation and connection with each other as you enjoy your meal. It is sadly missing in many homes.

Ken could testify to this fact. His single-parent mother seldom was home for supper. She did the best she could, but seldom did her schedule permit her being home from work in time for supper. Ken would make a sandwich and eat alone as he watched television. Bill, on the other hand, along with his three sisters and two brothers had a mom and dad whose work allowed them the joy of being home together around the supper time hour. After prayer, asking God's blessing upon the food, their table was a place of chatter, laughter, and even a teaching moment or two. It never was a place where discipline was meted out, with the exception of "the look" as the kids would call it. The supper table was a place of enjoyment and blessings. Ken loved coming to Bill's house for supper whenever he was invited. He made a vow to himself that his supper table would be like Bill's. Little did he dream of how much joy would be produced and memories made around his little supper table as a married man.

Your couple's and family worship time. God's Word is so precious that wise couples enjoy these special devotional times worshipping the Lord together. If you do not have children yet, or even if your children are grown and gone from your home, enjoy time with the Lord not only alone in your own personal Bible reading but also with your spouse. Couple's devotional time with the Lord will bless your marriage in ways that surprise you. It will help you to connect with your spouse on levels that only God Himself can produce.

If the Lord allows you to have children, family worship will be a special time of making memories and demonstrating to your children how precious the Lord is. They will learn how much He wishes to bless their family. This will be a time when preferably Dad as the spiritual leader of the home (Mom may have to take the lead if Dad is not a spiritual leader) reads and explains the Bible in age-appropriate gatherings. This is not a long drawn out sermon-like lecture. Rather, it will be brief, pointed, and hopefully employ a little variety to make it enjoyable for your children. Family prayer time follows this. What a great opportunity to be creative in leading the family in daily Bible reading.

Years ago my children were reflecting upon some of their best memories of our home and family. Every single one of our children talked about those family moments when we would meet later in the evening for family worship. They remembered family devotions and implemented them with their family.

Even if your children are grown and gone, you will be wise to commit to sitting at the supper table and actually talking, reflecting upon your day, and investing in each other. At some time during the day worship the Lord together. Intentionally make time to read the Scriptures and pray together. It is a wonderful time of following the Blueprint. It is so profitable.

The supper table and the family devotions, in addition to your own personal time in the Word of God, provide great opportunities for you and your family to learn more about God's Blueprint.

Know your Architect

The blueprint is certainly very important; however, it is equally important to get to know and understand the work of the architect personally. He or she will be very involved in the building of your beautiful house. If you built your house, perhaps you and your spouse met your architect and listened to his or her plan. He explained the many requirements and varied aspects of building your house. He should have answered your questions. He worked closely with your builders and contractors. Great architects design and oversee the construction of beautiful houses. It is the same with the great Architect, the Designer of your beautiful marriage.

Great builders know their architects and even enjoy an ongoing relationship with them. Do you know your Master Architect, the Lord Jesus Christ? By this, I mean, do you have a personal relationship with Him?

Do you know Him as your Savior? Many people know about the Lord but may not know Him in a personal and saving way.

So think about this. Has there been a time in your life that you have realized that you are a sinner and that your only hope of forgiveness is in the shedding of Christ's blood, His death and His resurrection? Powerfully the Lord Jesus reminds us, "But as many as received Him, to them He gave power to become the sons of God, even to them which believe on His name" (John 1:12).

Pastor Kenward asked this question to Ken and Alisha. The couple looked at the pastor and then at each other. Ken spoke first, "We went to church, gave money to the church, and even helped with a little remodeling project. But I do not remember ever being asked by the pastor in our previous church about a personal relationship with the Lord."

Alisha quickly chimed it, "That's right, but I do want this personal relationship you are talking about. I'm so glad we started attending this church. Mr. Mitchell told us about you and 'his' church. You talked to us about God's Word, and that's what we need."

That day Pastor Kenward introduced them to the Lord Jesus Christ, and they trusted Him as their personal Savior. Do you know the Lord?

Your relationship with Christ is absolutely vital. While it is very possible for couples who do not know the Lord to become best friends, that friendship will never compare to the friendship that the Lord Jesus Christ wants to bring into homes and marriages of His people. The Lord God is the great Architect and Engineer in the designing of wonderful marriages and Christian homes. What must you know about your Architect?

He alone is God

There is no one else like unto Him. He is totally opposite of the cultural and societal point of view. He holds a place held by none other. He is God. The Psalmist described it beautifully when he wrote, "But our God is in the Heavens; he hath done whatsoever He hath pleased" (Psalm 115:3). The prophet Isaiah declared, "Look unto me, and be ye saved, all the ends of the earth: for I am God, and there is none else" (Isaiah 45:22).

Our present culture at best sends confusing and outright disastrous messages to the American home. Some of these messages include the following:

- You deserve to be happy.
- You are the most important person in the world.
- Do whatever you want to find your own happiness.
- You must find happiness within yourself.
- Do not depend on others to find fulfillment.
- Everyone's concept of truth must be approved and accepted.

Current culture increasingly demands political correctness and inclusivism. It insists that Biblical statements made 2,000 years ago are irrelevant today and that everyone's point of view is correct. How foolish are the thoughts of those who do not know the Lord! Rather than loving and following the Blueprint of He Who designed marriage, the American home and family has been bombarded with lies and deception.

Constantly you will have to battle the unbiblical lies of your culture and world. It is a spiritual enemy that tries to drag you away from the Architect of your life. The Apostle John put it this way as he wrote, "Love not the world, neither the things that are in the world. If any man loves the world, the love of the Father is not in him. For all that is in the world, the lust of the flesh, and the lust of the eyes, and the pride of life, is not of the Father, but is of the world. And the world passeth away, and the lust thereof: but he that doeth the will of God abideth forever" (1John 2:15-17).

If you and your spouse are to stay best friends after the honeymoon's over, it is absolutely essential to settle the questions of what your marriage will be like and who will be in charge. You can have a good marriage without including the Lord, but I can guarantee that you will never have the greatest marriage you can have. You and your spouse must choose the Lord as the One Who is in charge of your lives and marriage.

As the Lord God, He greatly desires to share with you the joy of His Master Blueprint, the Scriptures. He is the Author and Designer of marriage, home, and family. He can turn your mediocre marriage into a great marriage. He can change your broken marriage into a blessed marriage. He specializes in fixing broken homes and families, one person at a time.

Think of this. What is your view of God? How would you describe the place He holds in your marriage?

He gives an invitation which is amazing
He is exclusive in that there are no others from whom you can choose. On the other hand, His invitation to come is very inclusive in that it is open to all who will accept His invitation. This is awesome. He is exclusive. He alone is God. Yet His invitation is inclusive. It is open to all. Millions have accepted the invitation "Come unto Me, all ye that labour and are heavy laden, and I will give you rest. Take My yoke upon you, and learn of Me: for I am meek and lowly in heart: and ye shall find rest unto your souls. For My yoke is easy, and My burden is light" (Matthew 11:28-30).

He reveals Himself as being awesome
Some would say that the word "awesome" is used far too flippantly today. You hear of awesome sports' moves, awesome automobiles, awesome paintings. Most everything today is labeled "awesome."

When you as a couple really begin to grasp how significant the Scriptures are in your marriage and how precious is the Lord, the Author and Designer of marriage, probably the word "awesome" will really come to your mind. Consider what Jeremiah had to say about this, "But the LORD is the true God, He is the living God, and an everlasting King: at His wrath the earth shall tremble, and the nation shall not be able to abide His indignation" (Jeremiah 10:10).

So the question that begs to be answered is, "What does God's Word mean to you as a couple?" Are you among the thousands of couples who have many Bibles in their homes, carry them faithfully to church on Sunday (when there is time to go!), and yet during the week seldom open and read the Bible with each other? Or are you, on the other hand, among the fewer couples who not only read the Bible on a regular basis individually but also read God's Word together as a couple? The outcome of the level of friendship in your marriage will be directly tied to the investment and the application of God's Word in your marriage and home.

Maybe it sounds rather simple to you. Read God's Word regularly. Accept it personally. Apply it consistently because your Architect is awesome and perfect in every way. This is where the building of your wonderful marriage begins. Have confidence in your Architect. He is awesome and perfect in all His ways.

Appreciate the Blueprint

God's Word is a very powerful tool that can change the worst marriage into a great marriage. While this will not take place overnight, God's Word is so amazing that it literally changes lives and marriages. Referring back to 2 Timothy 3:16-17, it is interesting to see how God's Word is profitable or useful in various stages of our lives. Consider what Paul says to his beloved son, Timothy, and to us.

It is profitable for doctrine

This speaks of what you must learn to believe (2 Timothy 3:16c). God has revealed wonderful truth about Himself and everything that you need to know for the present time. It will be incredible for you to learn what God has said about your marriage. It will be blessed to implement that precious set of teachings into your home.

1. What are several Biblical Blueprint teachings about yourself that you are putting into application today?

2. What are several Biblical Blueprint teachings about your marriage that you are putting into application today?

It is profitable for reproof

Reproof gives the idea of that which brings about conviction when you have thought or acted improperly (2 Timothy 3:16d). As you read God's Word, there will be moments when most likely you will stop, put your finger on the reference, and sense the Lord's conviction. This dramatic and personal confrontation occurs when you realize that you have fallen short of God's standard and design in the Master Blueprint. With this comes the emotion of feeling sorry that you have fallen short, hurt the Lord and perhaps disappointed your loved one. This sorrow brings a change of mind which is called repentance.

1. Are there specific times in your life that you have sensed such repentance as you read God's Word?

2. How have you acted upon such times? Have you acknowledged your sin to the Lord and your spouse and sought forgiveness?

3. Are you more apt to make excuses for your actions or genuinely ask for forgiveness?

It is profitable for correction

Though closely tied to reproof, correction is slightly different. It is wonderful to understand this beautiful word picture. Correction speaks of a person falling flat on his face and being picked up and restored to an upright position. You have experienced this, haven't you?

There will be times that you realize that you have sinned and fallen flat again (2 Timothy 3:16e). When you have stumbled, fallen or wandered away, God's Word restores you to an upright position as you apply what you read. When heeded, it is amazing how God's Word corrects that which previously was broken or crooked.

1. Honestly evaluate your life. Are there any broken areas in your life or relationship?

2. If so, do you know what God's Word says about these broken areas? Do you know how to apply God's Word to these areas?

It is profitable for instruction in righteousness

Powerfully and practically God's Word teaches you how to live as a child of the Lord. He has given clear directions instructing how you can be righteous in your marriage, in your parenting, and in the affairs of your household (2 Timothy 3:16f). It is wonderful to understand that God does not expect you to be perfect. He does, however, expect you to be righteous!

Adhere to the Blueprint

So, what does the Lord, the awesome Architect and Designer of the Master Blueprint have to say about your marriage? What are some of the things to implement in your home to make your marriage a great and growing friendship? For now, consider just a couple basic things. These are what that the Lord Jesus said about your marriage in Matthew 19. Find your Bible and invest some profitable time in God's Word.

The priority of your spouse

"For this cause shall a man leave father and mother, and shall cleave to his wife" (19:5a). The idea of cleaving is being permanently glued to each other. This of course does not mean that you will never be physically away from your spouse. It does mean that your spouse will always be present in your heart.

The priority of your partnership

"And they twain [two] shall be one flesh" (19:5b). This is not going to come automatically. The oneness of flesh is more than just the physical intimacy of husband and wife. This speaks as well of the emotional intimacy that comes through thoughtfulness, kindness, and love expressed. As you and your spouse read the Word of God together, as well as pray for each other, it will be amazing how your love will grow. Your marriage will even become more enjoyable than you could imagine.

The priority of God working in your lives

"What therefore God hath joined together" (19:6a). The Lord greatly desires to be part of your lives and marriage. When He is invited into your marriage, it will be amazing what changes He brings. When He is invited to be in charge of your marriage, it is precious to see what blessings He sends. You and your spouse have a great opportunity to intentionally ask Him to be the Lord of your lives and marriage. You'll be glad you did.

The Psalmist wrote, "The works of the LORD are great, sought out of all them that have pleasure in them. His work is honorable and glorious: and His righteousness endureth for ever. He hath made His wonderful works to be remembered: the LORD is gracious and full of compassion" (Psalm 111:2-4).

This is a great place to stop and write out some of the blessings that the Lord has worked out in your marriage. What has He done for you and your spouse up to now?

The priority of implementing safety guardrails

"Let not man put asunder" (19:6b). In other words, you need good guardrails to keep you from crashing down a slope into great destruction. The Lord Jesus very clearly states that you must never allow anyone or anything to endanger or harm your marriage. Fantasies entertained, impurities thought upon, unwholesome images viewed, and flirtations lived out pose serious threats and dangers to you and your marriage. These dangers can be avoided and overcome by adhering to the Master Blueprint. What safety and blessings are found by implementing the warnings of the Blueprint, the Scriptures! God's Word is sufficient and effective in safeguarding your home and marriage.

Knowing your Architect personally and placing your confidence in His Blueprint is a good start. For lasting changes to take place in your marriage and for you and your spouse to become best friends, you both must commit to following the Master Blueprint.

Think about these questions

1. Do you and your mate understand what it means to know the Lord Jesus as your personal Savior?

2. What is your goal for reading God's Word during the week?
   _____ Nearly everyday
   _____ Three or four times per week
   _____ Once or twice per week.
   _____ Seldom during the week

3. How could your schedule be changed slightly to accommodate a few minutes to read God's Word on a regular basis?

4. Do you and your spouse read God's Word together throughout the week? If not regularly, what are some of the things that keep you from it?

Take the challenge of committing to following the Master Blueprint, the Bible. Have the goal of reading it daily, memorizing it earnestly, practicing it consistently, and living it beautifully. Don't settle for an average or mediocre marriage. God's Word, the Master Blueprint, when followed will build a beautiful marriage.

The Precious Word of God

How amazing is the thought
that He who spoke and brought creation into existence,
that He Who stretches the universe by His power,
that He who measures the earth's water by the handfuls,
is the One who wishes to speak to me!
Who am I that the Lord of all glory
should ever call me by my name and speak to me
of things that are grand beyond all measure?
Who am I that the Lord of all glory awaits my coming in the morning
and desires me to conclude my day with His precious
Word in the evening?
Who am I? I cannot comprehend this!
But I will give thanks and praise Him.
I will read His Word with expectation and gratitude.
With His help, I will implement it in my marriage.
I will become the person He has designed and desires.
I am excited to see what my marriage can become.
I want to grow and cherish my spouse as my best friend,
just as the great Architect has designed.
By His grace I shall do this. Best friends with my spouse and
Him as my Lord will be my greatest joy.

It is my prayer that there will be a little "dust" which is the evidence that you are working in this area in your marriage. Constructing a beautiful marriage is a lot like constructing a beautiful house!

Chapter Four
Building Upon a Great Foundation

Anything Else is Absolutely Foolish

"Therefore whosoever heareth these sayings of mine,
and doeth them, I will liken him unto a wise man
which built his house upon a rock: And the rain descended,
and the floods came, and the winds blew, and beat upon that house;
and it fell not; for it was founded upon a rock.
And every one that heareth these sayings of mine,
and doeth them not,
shall be likened unto a foolish man, which built his house upon the sand:
And the rain descended, and the floods came, and the winds blew,
and beat upon that house;
and it fell: and great was the fall of it"
(Matthew 7:24-27)

Sand is beautiful to walk upon,
but when it comes to building sturdy structures,
be sure that you are building on a rock!
Sand is excellent for the long stretches of beach to walk upon,
but a rock is the kind of foundation to build upon.
There will be storms.
Foundations of sand crumble.
Foundations of rock hold the house securely.

From Grandpa's note: Build upon a good solid foundation. You don't want to fall apart when storms come.

———

Key thought: *A foundation provides the support upon which buildings are built. The key to a strong and secure structure is to build on an exceedingly solid and proven foundation. The key to building a strong and secure marriage is to build on the solid, proven Word of God.*

The day came for Ken and Alisha that the builders would be laying the foundation of their house. Ken took the day off, and they enjoyed watching the concrete being poured. It was hard to imagine what their brand new house would look like. One of the Mitchell brothers came over to them as they watched the crew.

"Come here, you two," Sam Mitchell told them. "Bend down right here. Ken, you press your left hand in the cement. Push a little harder. That's good. All right, Miss Alisha, you come here and press your right hand so that your right thumbprint touches Ken's left thumbprint," Sam said.

The couple complied. Wiping their hands off with a rag supplied by Sam, they looked down at the prints of their hands. Sam smiled at them, and then spoke seriously to them, "Ken and Alisha, though your house will be built up around these prints, you will always remember that these prints are here. It's kind of like you folks will always remember that your house is built upon a great foundation, just like the Lord talked about."

They never forgot that day. How thankful they both were that they had hired Mitchell and Sons Construction!

Christ's Application

What a vivid application to conclude our Lord's sermon! The Lord Jesus preached His great Sermon on the Mount as recorded in Matthew chapters five through seven. Can't you just picture the Lord Jesus standing on the grassy slopes on the northwest corner of the Sea of Galilee? Multitudes gathered to listen to Him. When He came to the conclusion of His powerful sermon, He summarized His message with the illustration of two men building two different houses on two different foundations with two different outcomes.

The foolish man
The man is said to be foolish because he built his house upon the sand (Matthew 7:26). When it comes to building, it is hard to imagine someone being so foolish as to build his house on that which shifts and blows away. Sure enough, the storms came, and when the rain and wind beat upon that house, it fell flat.

What constitutes a man being foolish today? The Lord Jesus teaches us that anyone who hears God's Word and does not do it is a foolish man. What great and devastating loss because of his disregard for God's Word, the proper foundation!

The wise man
On the other hand, another man chose his foundation carefully and is said to be wise. This man built his house upon the rock. He knew that building a long-lasting house would require the proper sturdy foundation. What is this foundation? The Lord Jesus explains that when we hear God's Word and obey it, we will be wise, and our house, which is our life, will stand firm even against the most violent of storms.

Picture the two men, the two houses and the two outcomes
The illustration of the two men that are building two different houses with two different outcomes concludes the Sermon on the Mount in a powerful and practical way. It is the closing illustration that leaves a lasting impression. It is easily understood. After hearing the Word of God, a choice between obedience and disobedience must be made. Obedience is the wise course of action. It builds a house, a life, that stands. Disobedience is the foolish course of action. Destruction and heartache are sure to follow.

In the previous chapter we thought about our Architect and the blessing of understanding that the Blueprint He has designed is perfect and useful. There is great joy in being confident in it. Now you and your spouse must build on this by understanding that Christ's words are the foundation upon which you build your lives and marriage.

Christ's Authority on Three Important Issues of Life

Catch the full impact of the wording of our Savior as He says, "Whosoever heareth these sayings of mine, and doeth them, I will liken him unto a wise man" (Matthew 7:24). There are many voices that clamor for your attention. They absolutely insist that they know better how to build a marriage. Listen again with confidence to the voice of your Savior as He talks about His words and those who listen and obey. He is the Authority on building a marriage that stays best friends long after the honeymoon's over. Choose to listen to Him!

Read His Word, and you will discover that the Lord Jesus spoke about many things relating to your personal life. It would be interesting to take time to read through the Sermon on the Mount (Matthew 5-7) and read His teachings. In the next few pages, you and your spouse will be confronted with three of the things Christ spoke about in His awesome sermon. He spoke about many important issues; however, these three are selected because, sadly, all three of these things routinely impact homes and marriages today. The words of our Savior focus on anger, adultery, and divorce.

Anger is the outflow of hostility and resentment. Instead of building bridges to each other, angry spouses build walls which push each other away. Words that are spoken in anger result in great emotional wounds. Often these are more painful than a physical blow.

The act of adultery is super-destructive. It shatters marriages as it blows apart the bridge built between the spouses. Equally as devastating and becoming much more common is the "adultery of the heart" of which the Lord Jesus speaks. Pornography is rampant and has become the secret sin in the typically fine local church. It's no longer just an issue impacting men. More and more women are becoming addicted to pornography.

Divorce is thought to be the easiest option to follow when marital problems arise. It severs family ties. Children suffer such loss and sorrow because of divorce. Though God allowed it in the Old Testament times because of the hardness of the human heart, He has a wonderful plan for marriage today. Divorce is not the option of choice for those couples who commit to following the Word of God.

Think through several of the statements of our Savior and how they apply to your marriage. Remember, it is the wise man who listens and obeys His words.

He speaks about anger and murder

We are not robots. We have a full set of wide-ranging emotions. Anger is one of those emotions, and the Lord Jesus spoke about this.

Think about what He said. "Ye have heard that it was said by them of old time, Thou shalt not kill; and whosoever shall kill shall be in danger of the judgment: But I say unto you, that whosoever is angry with his brother without a cause shall be in danger of the judgment: and whosoever shall say to his brother, Raca, shall be in danger of the council: but whosoever shall say, Thou fool, shall be in danger of hell fire" (Matthew 5:21-22).

Think of His words as He spoke about being angry with a brother without a cause. The word He selected for angry is *orgizo* (or-GE-zo) which has to do with "a provocation, an arousal of agitation and wrath." It probably is nearly impossible to live around people, even from a distance, without being provoked from time to time. It surely is not possible to live in close proximity to those at home without being provoked once in a while.

Anger and murder are closely related

Now the Lord Jesus takes this interpersonal fracture another step by talking to them about their anger and relating it to murder! The people to whom He was speaking knew they were not to commit murder. For decades they had been taught from the Old Testament that murder was a great sin and therefore forbidden. How amazed they must have been when they heard the Lord Jesus say something like, "Not only do I not want you to murder someone, I do not want you to be angry without a cause at that person. Your anger makes you murderers." Talk about an attention grabber!

Do you have trouble with anger? How excellent is our Savior and Teacher. He teaches about your anger by comparing it with a fire that starts small. If left unchecked, it quickly grows stronger and becomes bigger. He explains to His listeners that if they have inner feelings of unchecked anger, that is cause for a local or provincial court to hear that case (5:22a).

If their anger grows and breaks out into an expression of scorn, "Raca", (which means "stupid, empty-headed"), that is cause to be heard by the council or the Sanhedrin. Anger that culminates in an explosion of abusiveness and derogatory language, "You fool!" is punishable directly by the Lord!

What an interesting revelation the Lord Jesus makes as to the danger of anger! How it can greatly affect your marriage and home! It often starts out over something little or insignificant. If not dealt with, it certainly can grow in intensity, resulting in words that are hurtful and wounding to relationships. If left still unchecked, this anger can explode in a furious eruption, much like a spewing volcano.

A practical illustration
Think of Lorinda's situation. She easily becomes annoyed with her husband, Tony. Usually it is over seemingly small and insignificant things. Saturday afternoon Tony came in from working on the landscaping of their home. She had asked him "a million times" to be sure to wash his hands in the laundry room just inside the garage door.

Once again Tony forgot. Careless, thoughtless Tony! Coming into the kitchen to get a drink of water, Tony left a couple of dirty fingerprints on the counter top. Though it was thoughtless, it did not rise to the seriousness of Loretta's anger. She shouted and called him "stupid."

Following him out of the kitchen and chasing him onto the deck, she shouted to him at the top of her voice. "Can't you ever do anything right?" she screamed. "When I make your supper, I now have to wash my counter tops again. Why do you always make a mess? You never do what I want you to do!" were her last venomous words before she turned around, walked inside and slammed the door. Lorinda opened the door one more time and screamed, "You always make messes. You drive me crazy. I hate you."

Those two "trigger" words
Did you catch the two trigger words? They are "always" and "never." Often these are the trigger words fired in heated discussions of anger. Combine

these words with the volume and tone of voice and they can be deadly in their wounding capacity.

Obviously Lorinda has an anger problem. As the target of her anger, Tony also has a problem with anger—her name is Lorinda.

Don't misunderstand. Not all anger is sinful. In fact, the Scriptures teach that there is an appropriate time for the right amount of anger and the right duration of anger. Anger is a hot emotion. That is why the Scriptures lay heavy restrictions upon anger. It must be for the right reason. It must be for the right duration. It always must be in the right amount.

The Apostle Paul gave tremendous counsel in Ephesians 4:26. Providing instruction for the church at Ephesus, he wrote, "Be ye angry, and sin not: let not the sun go down upon your wrath: neither give place to the devil" (Ephesians 4:26-27). Think of these words. Anger needs to be dealt with and put away by sunset. If you tend to be an angry person, you no doubt hate the winter months because sunset arrives so early. Angry people enjoy the longer days of light that come in summer because it gives them longer to hold out forgiveness! Seriously, anger is a serious emotion that needs to be controlled and dealt with as soon as possible. The results of not dealing with anger are harmful indeed.

An extremely important moment

Stop and honestly ask yourself, "Am I an angry person?" How do you think others would answer that question about you?

Do you find yourself at times being easily frustrated and very explosive? Do your emotions run high and frequently get agitated? The Apostle Paul provides great counsel for you to deal with anger issues. Powerfully he tells the Ephesian believers, "Let no corrupt communication proceed out of your mouth…And grieve not the Holy Spirit of God, whereby ye are sealed unto the day of redemption. Let all bitterness, and wrath, and anger, and clamor, and evil speaking, be put away from you, with all malice." (Ephesians 4:29-31). Think about that list.

- ***Corrupt communication*** (4:29) This gives the picture of rotten, decaying, and foul language deliberately hurled at another. Words that are used as weapons by angry people demonstrate that the old adage "sticks and stones may break my bones, but words can never hurt me" is the biggest lie in the world. Sticks and stones hurt much less than words that hurt emotionally. The hurt from sticks and stones eventually heals, whereas the pain of hurtful words can last a lifetime.

- **Bitterness** (4:31a) This is the fruit that grows from the root of grudges long held onto. Such fruit is poisonous, distasteful and unhealthy (Hebrews 12:15). Do you struggle with bitterness? Do you find yourself hanging on to the hurts that you have experienced from others? Is it robbing you of the joy that the Lord Jesus wants you to experience? The Apostle Paul says, "Let it be put away."

- **Wrath** (4:31b) If you live nearby a person of "wrath," you know it is an explosive emotion that flares up or erupts without much warning. It is loud and calls attention to the person who is often shouting, banging fists, or even kicking feet. Is this ever a description of you at times? It is important to remember that no one living near an explosion of wrath goes unaffected. The destructive emotional wounds are deep and lasting. Do you act out in wrath at times? The Apostle Paul says, "Let it be put away."

- **Anger** (4:31c) This is the strong passion of agitation and displeasure. It can last for long periods of time when not given over to the Lord. Angry people tend to attract other angry people. What a growing problem develops because their anger feeds off each other! Both are miserable, and those living nearby feel their misery as well. Lasting and loving relationships are often ruined because of the anger of one or both spouses. You may not consider yourself an angry person, but would others say that you have anger issues?

You may have been wounded unjustly. While you may never completely forget the hurts you have experienced, you don't have to carry your anger with you. Perhaps you have carried this wound or hurt for many years. This anger has become a flame that will burn a hole in emotions and actions, as well as seriously hurt those who love you. If you are angry, the Apostle Paul says, "Let it be put away."

- ***Clamour*** (4:31d) What an interesting word "clamour" is. The Scriptural word "clamour" is *krauge*. This gives the idea of someone who "makes an outcry and creates controversy." Picture someone who is loud and agitates constantly. This person tends to add fuel to the fire when it comes to an injustice.

  It is interesting how some folks are able to calm a situation down by the way they speak and conduct themselves. Their words are soothing, and their very presence is calming. Other folks are the opposite. They ignite and agitate the situation by their careless actions and poorly chosen words. These folks stoke the flames of the offense and act as an accelerant by their clamorous words. Do you wrestle with this? If so, the Apostle Paul says, "Let it be put away."

- ***Evil speaking*** (4:31e) These two words form our present word "blasphemy." This focuses on a slanderous, injurious language that hurts and defames others. It is the kind of communication that cuts people down, hurts reputations, and makes others think less of a person. Isn't it amazing how easy it is for our words to be evil? Do you catch yourself immediately thinking the worst of people? Do you almost automatically say things that just are not helpful? Which is it? Do you tend to build others up, or do you tend to tear them down? If you are prone to speak in an evil way of people or situations, the Apostle Paul says, "Let it be put away."

- ***Malice*** (4:31f). What a silent wickedness is malice, which lies just below the surface. It is often undetected by others. It is ill will or the silent wicked desire to see someone hurt or harmed. It harbors the desire for getting even or being revengeful for past hurts inflicted. Do you ever harbor malice? If so, the Apostle Paul says, "Let it be put away."

Did you notice how destructive anger and its wicked cousins, corrupt communication, bitterness, wrath, clamour, evil speaking, and malice are in a marriage relationship? No wonder we read that the Holy Spirit is grieved (Ephesians 4:30) at such things. Build a great marriage on the sure foundation of hearing Christ's words and doing them. Get rid of anger and its evil cousins.

Understanding and dealing with your anger

How do you get rid of anger? Assuming that you have placed your trust in Christ as Savior, there are several things to consistently do to overcome sinful anger.

- ***Confess it as sin*** (1 John 1:9). Agree with the Lord and acknowledge that you are viewing this as sin. Don't offer excuses. Don't blame others. Be honest with the Lord and yourself. View your anger as the Lord views it.

- ***Learn to speak the truth in love*** (Ephesians 4:15) by carefully practicing how to talk to others. Be truthful. Be honest. Ask the Lord Jesus to control your anger and replace it with His calmness. Don't speak until the Lord has calmed you down and you have had sufficient time to think about the choice of your words.

  Truthful words communicated in a loving, calm, and gentle manner are the opposite of the hurtful words of anger. Through the Holy Spirit, ask Him to grow His precious fruit in your life. He describes it as "love, joy, peace, longsuffering, gentleness, goodness, faith, meekness, and temperance" (Galatians 5:22-23).

- ***Ask the Lord to help you to begin to think in a renewed way*** (Ephesians 4:23). Paul the Apostle describes this as deliberately *putting off* the ways of the old man (4:22) and *putting on* the ways of the new man (4:24). This is accomplished through the renewed thinking the Holy Spirit is able to give. It comes about through memorizing God's Word (Psalm 119:9, 11) and the deliberate, intentional 'stop and think before you speak' kind of communication.

- ***Take seriously the directive as to how to handle anger*** (4:26). Even anger for the right reason has limits. It is never to be demonstrated or communicated by the list of sinful words through which you have read. The Apostle Paul spoke of not letting the sun go down upon an anger problem. That speaks to us of the importance of dealing with it quickly. Do not allow it to fester and build. It is to be dealt with, and as Paul would say, "Let it be put away from you" (4:31). Replace it with "And be ye kind one to another, tenderhearted, forgiving one another, even as God for Christ's sake hath forgiven you" (4:32).

Anger hurled at a loved one always harms a marriage. Living with an angry spouse makes the marriage miserable. The writer of Proverbs puts it this way, "It is better to dwell in the wilderness than with a contentious and angry woman." To stay best friends long after the honeymoon's over, anger must be put away.

If you or a loved one are dealing with the effects of anger in your marriage, understand that anger is a dangerous weapon that wounds deeply those who are the target.

Take a few moments to look up these verses, and in your own words write about the application or how these verses speak to you.

- Proverbs 14:17
- Proverbs 22:24
- Proverbs 29:22
- Ecclesiastes 7:9

You are building upon the great foundation which requires your consistent hearing and obeying the words of the Lord Jesus concerning your anger.

Christ's Authority on Adultery and Lust

What grave dangers lurk in the mind of those who entertain lustful fantasies. Often such fantasy leads to adultery. Think about what the Lord Jesus said. "Ye have heard that it was said by them of old time, Thou shalt not commit adultery: But I say unto you, That whosoever looketh on a woman to lust after her hath committed adultery with her already in his heart" (Matthew 5:27-28).

The Old Testament Law

Under the Old Testament Law of Moses, sex outside of marriage was strictly forbidden. Period. The people to whom the Lord Jesus was speaking understood what He meant by the commandment, "Ye shall not commit adultery," which referred back to the seventh commandment found in Exodus 20:14. It is clear. It is straightforward. It is non-negotiable. Adultery under any circumstance results in heartache, loss, and deep regret (2 Samuel 11-12).

His present expansion and application

The Lord Jesus explained and expanded His application of this commandment to a far deeper dimension. Not only is the actual physical act of adultery forbidden, but also the lustful fantasy of imagination is forbidden. He uses two very interesting words when speaking about looking and lusting. The looking is *blepo* which has the idea of "to perceive, to take heed." The word for lust is *epithumeo* which gives the picture of "to long for, to greatly desire."

Obviously the Lord Jesus is not speaking about a quick, casual glance of a lady passing by in our line of sight. He does not expect men to keep their eyes closed throughout the day. This situation of which the Lord Jesus is speaking is rather the deliberate pause, the gaze, the fixation and the fantasy of imagining that which is forbidden. It may not be the actual act of adultery, but it is in the desire or imagination of what might be.

Some would argue that such fantasizing is not a serious problem; however, that is not what the Lord Jesus teaches. Clearly He instructed the people in His great Sermon on the Mount that the lustful look may not be the actual deed of adultery, but it is the wicked desire of adultery (Matthew 5:27-28). According to the Lord Jesus, adultery can take place in your heart through what lingers in your thoughts and mind.

The precious gift of intimacy

A healthy marriage where friendship grows strong long after the honeymoon's over is my prayer for every reader. One of the ways that this precious marital friendship grows is by the wonderful expression of sexual intimacy. Sexual love between one man and one woman united in marriage for a lifetime is a tremendous gift from God (Hebrew 13:4).

Think about these questions

1. Are you finding satisfaction in the present level of intimacy within your marriage? If the answer is no, what is causing your lack of satisfaction?

2. Is your spouse finding fulfillment in the present level of intimacy within your marriage? If the answer is no, what is causing your spouse's lack of satisfaction?

3. What do you think are some things that keep couples from sexual fulfillment?

4. Are you experiencing any of these things? If so, what are you doing to address them?

5. Immoral fantasizing and lustful desires diminish and destroy the wonderful intimacy that God desires in a healthy marriage. Is this a problem in your marriage?

We live in a wonderful age of technology, and we certainly enjoy the great benefits such technology brings to us. But with the wonderful blessings of technology comes a very wicked and ever present temptation. Online pornography is easily and readily available. Though many believe that it is harmless, the opposite is true. The viewing of pornography clearly is sinful, according to the Lord Jesus (Matthew 5:28). It is degrading to those who pose for its pictures, and it is destructive for those who view them.

Good ministries that help those with the sin of pornography all consistently affirm that this is *not* a situation that is isolated outside of the church. These ministries affirm that within good local church families a significant percentage of those attending on any given Sunday have purposefully viewed pornography during the week. Be assured that if you or your spouse find pleasure in pornographic sites, your marriage will indeed suffer, and the friendship aspect of your relationship will be greatly damaged.

There is nothing like the intimacy of the husband and wife who view their bodies as given only to each other and the act of intimacy reserved for them alone. This beautiful, honorable intimacy is broken when one spouse or both seeks to find pleasure and excitement in pornography.

What if there is a reason that hinders sexual intimacy? It is important to understand that intimacy can still occur, even if there is a physical reason why sexual intercourse cannot take place. Occasionally, as couples age, there are physical reasons why couples can no longer function in the act of marriage; however, they still can be intimate. This comes from the holding, hugging, caressing, and assurance that you are reserved for each other as long as life shall last.

Wise words written

Proverbs 5 provides clear and very practical instructions for those who wrestle with adulterous ways and lustful thoughts. Whether the adultery is being committed in person with another or if it is taking place in your thoughts alone, either way it will destroy the wonderful gift of intimacy and the joy of sexuality in your marriage. Think of what Solomon said to his son.

- ***Take this seriously.*** Purity of heart and the deliverance from sexual impurity must be taken very seriously (5:1-2). The writer of the book of Proverbs greatly desires his son to pay attention and listen to his admonition. Is this an area of your life in which you have been wrestling? Perhaps you secretly are trying to protect your actions, assuming that you will never be caught. If this is true, overcoming it and returning to moral purity begins with taking it seriously. It starts with saying, "No," and making provision for a whole new way of living.

- ***Don't be fooled.*** Sexual sin often wraps itself beautifully and presents itself attractively (5:3). Though it may appear to be greatly enticing, the end result is far from beautiful. Solomon speaks of it as being "bitter as wormwood and sharp as a two-edged sword." The wormwood speaks of it being noxious and poisonous. The two-edged sword speaks of its great destruction.

- ***Danger ahead!*** Flirting with the possibility of sexual sin is a dangerous road, and you will be wise to avoid it (5:5-8). Solomon warns his son to build safeguards to keep him from the ways of sexual impurity. The good counsel of advising his son to avoid even coming near the door of her house is a way of erecting wise safeguards. If your marriage is to grow in its friendship long after the honeymoon's over, you must establish strong safeguards to protect you both from the way of sexual immorality. It may look beautiful and enticing, but it will result in great bitterness that will harm and threaten intimacy in your marriage.

- ***Remember this little formula.*** Never forget the 20/20 principle. Twenty minutes of passion and pleasure will never be worth the twenty years of misery and heartache (5:9-14). You and your spouse

Building Upon a Great Foundation

will be very wise to heed this simple admonition that Solomon gave to his son. He likens the end result of sexual sin to the person who has worked hard for his wealth and suddenly throws it away, giving to others the profit of his labor. The warning is clear and powerful. Don't throw away the wonderful gift you have been given, intimacy with your spouse throughout your lifetime, by giving it to another.

- ***Choose wisely.*** Keep your marriage beautiful as you grow in your love and remain faithful to your commitment to sexual purity (5:15-20). Solomon speaks in vivid illustrations clearly understood by his son. Drinking waters out of your own cistern (5:15), rejoicing with the wife of your youth (5:18), and finding satisfaction and joy in sexual intimacy with your spouse (5:19-20) are the ways to stay best friends when the honeymoon's long over.

Take a few moments to look up the following verses, and in your own words write the application of each verse. Think of what God has to say about sinful lust and how we are to deal with it in this world.

- 1 John 2:15-17
- Ephesians 2:1-3
- Colossians 3:5-7
- Titus 2:11-12
- 2 Timothy 2:22

The Apostle Paul reminded the Corinthian believers of their past lives. He said, "Know ye not that the unrighteous shall not inherit the kingdom of God? Be not deceived: neither fornicators, nor idolaters, nor adulterers, nor effeminate, nor abusers of themselves with mankind, nor thieves, nor covetous, nor drunkards, nor revilers, nor extortioners, shall inherit the kingdom of God. And such were some of you" (1 Corinthians 6:9-11a).

The Corinthian believers once lived wickedly. Sexual sin was rampant, but then a wonderful thing took place in their lives. They each came to know the Lord Jesus Christ as their personal Savior, and they were changed. Paul goes on to describe them, "But ye are sanctified, but ye are justified in the name of the Lord Jesus, and by the Spirit of our God (1 Corinthians 6:11b).

Every house that endures began by being built upon a great foundation. Hearing the words of our Lord Jesus and doing them likens us to being the wise man who built his house upon the rock. You can never have lasting, joyful intimacy the way God intended it to be if either you or your spouse lives in a world of lust and sexual fantasy. The boundaries established by our great God are not prison walls. They are guardrails to keep us from sure harm and grave danger.

Christ's Authority on Divorce

Divorce always results in a terrible fracture. Listen to the words of our blessed Savior as He speaks to the crowds in his great Sermon on the Mount. He said, "It hath been said, Whosoever shall put away his wife, let him give her a writing of divorcement: But I say unto you, that whosoever shall put away his wife, saving for the cause of fornication, causes her to commit adultery: and whosoever shall marry her that is divorced committeth adultery (Matthew 5:31-32).

The Old Testament economy

Repeatedly the Lord Jesus rehearsed what the Old Testament Mosaic Law demanded. Moses spelled out that divorce and remarriage were permitted under certain circumstances, according to Deuteronomy 24:1-4. The Lord Jesus explained that divorce was allowed in the Old Testament economy because of the hardness of people's hearts. He said, "Moses because of the hardness of your hearts suffered you to put away your wives: but from the beginning it was not so" (Matthew 19:8).

When the Lord Jesus gave the exception clause of fornication, many Bible teachers believe that this 'divorce' was the breaking of their engagement, not the ending of the actual marriage. Their view of fornication is that that sexual sin took place between unmarried people during the engagement stage of their marriage. When fornication took place under those circumstances, a writing of divorcement would be granted, thus ending the engagement.

Please understand that no marriage is perfect. Neither you nor your spouse can ever expect your marriage to be perfect. Even the very best of marriages requires work on both the parts of the husband and wife. You may be going through a difficult period of time right now in your marriage. Perhaps you and your spouse are working on rebuilding a beautiful marriage just as if you were rebuilding your house. If you are honest, it is quite possible that you have entertained the thought that maybe it would just be easier to get a divorce and move on with your life. All this work at trying to rebuild a marriage and becoming the spouse that God intends you to be may at times be overwhelming. Never think that divorce is going to be the less painful route to go.

Deplorable condition in Malachi's time

Understanding the wonderful and unique unity of marriage is a great blessing. Malachi, the writer of the last book of the Old Testament, described with great heartache the deplorable condition of marriage in his time. He wrote, "And this have ye done again, covering the altar of the Lord with tears, with weeping, and with crying out, insomuch that He regarded not the offering anymore, or receiveth it with goodwill from your hand. Yet you say, Wherefore? Because the Lord hath been witness between thee and the wife of thy youth, against whom thou hast dealt treacherously: yet is she thy companion, and the wife of thy covenant" (Malachi 2:13-15).

Malachi gave a charge especially to the husbands to view their wives as being their "companion and the wife of his covenant" (2:14). The idea of "companion" is *chabereth* which gives the idea of being "united, a fellow, and one of deep association." From the side of Adam, near to his heart, Eve was taken. She and every wife since her would be the completion of her husband. Without her, something would be missing from his life. She is the one that is united, to walk with him in the closest association possible.

The word "covenant" is *beriyth,* which gives the idea of "the pledge of a lifetime." Marriage is not a contract which has loopholes and ways to get out of it. Contracts are conditional. If certain conditions are met, then certain agreements will be fulfilled. However, if those certain agreements are not met, the contractual agreement is rendered null and void. How different is a covenant. Marriage is a covenant in which the husband and wife pledge their love in the giving of their lives to each other. Because marriage is a covenant of companionship, divorce must be unthinkable.

Malachi referred to the act of divorce by these husbands as being an act of dealing treacherously. A covenant that is broken results in irreparable wounds that last a lifetime. Often the children of the divorcing parents are the ones that suffer the greatest. They are torn between their parents, both of whom they love. Often they blame themselves, believing that either they are the cause of the divorce or at least they should have prevented it.

Regardless of what our present culture suggests, marriage is between one man and one woman for one lifetime. God is the Designer of marriage. He sets the standards for marriage. He truly desires to help you to achieve the marriage that He is pleased to bless. Divorce should never be an option.

Take a few moments and read the following verses. In your own words, write out how these verses can be applied to your own marriage.

- Genesis 2:18
- Genesis 2:24-25
- Hebrews 13:4
- Ephesians 5:21

Christ and His Church

When the Apostle Paul wrote about marriage to the church of Ephesus, he presented a tremendous truth. It is not only a wonderful blessing to have a Godly marriage, it is also a great opportunity to demonstrate something special. The husband and wife relationship presents a beautiful picture of Christ and His church.

The wife and the church. The loving and Godly wife is represented by the love and respect demonstrated by the church to Christ, the Head, according to the Apostle Paul (Ephesians 5:22-24). The wife's submission is not out of dread and terror. It is rather the deep respect for her Godly husband demonstrated in her loving walk at his side.

What wonderful love and respect flows from the heart of the wife who knows she is cherished. Her husband not only says that he loves her, his actions also demonstrate that he loves her. He honors her and cherishes her in every way.

The husband and Christ. In a similar manner, the loving and Godly husband illustrates the role of the Lord and His incredible commitment to His church (Ephesians 5:25-31). He loves her (5:25a), gave Himself for her (5:25b), sets her apart unto Himself, gives her a place held by none other (5:26a), and cleanses her with the washing of His Word (5:25c).

This presents the powerful truth that the husband treats his wife in such a way as to keep her from resentment and bitterness. He presents to himself a glorious wife (5:27). What a beautiful way of saying they stayed best friends long after the honeymoon's over!

Christ's solid foundation

In all three of these critical issues of anger, adultery, and divorce, the Lord reminded the people of what the Old Testament Law demanded. They understood. Then He expanded and explained the situation by saying, "But I say unto you."

The Old Testament Law prohibited murder. The Lord Jesus stated, "But I say unto you whosoever is angry with his brother without a cause…" (Matthew 5: 21-22). The Old Testament Law prohibited adultery. The Lord Jesus stated, "But I say unto you that whosoever looks on a woman to lust after her hath committed adultery with her already in his heart (Matthew 5:27-28). The Old Testament Law allowed divorce. The Lord Jesus stated, "But I say unto you that whosoever shall put away his wife, saving for the cause of fornication, causes her to commit adultery: and whosoever shall marry her that is divorced commits adultery" (Matthew 5:32).

Go back to the laying of the firm foundation. Remember that the Lord Jesus explained that "Whosoever heareth these sayings of mine and doeth them, I will liken him unto a wise man which built his house upon a rock. The Lord Jesus has spoken, and those who are wise will listen and heed His words. Be wise and build upon a great foundation. Heed His words about anger, adultery, and divorce. Of course there are many other 'words of our Savior' that you and your spouse must hear and obey than just the three listed. Dealing with these three issues, however, is key to building your marriage upon a great Foundation.

What about the foolish man

You have been reading about the great and sturdy foundation upon which the wise person builds his house. As you remember, the storm came with the wind beating upon that house, and it stood firm because it was built upon a great foundation. The Lord Jesus explained in the concluding message of his great Sermon on the Mount that the Foundation is He Himself, and the wise person is the one who not only hears His words but also applies them to his own life and in obedience complies!

What about the foolish man who built his life upon the sand, which is recorded in Matthew 7:26-27, where the Lord Jesus says, "And everyone that heareth these sayings of mine, and doeth them not, shall be likened unto a foolish man, which built his house upon the sand: and the rains descended, and the floods came, and the winds blew, and beat upon that house, and it fell, and great was the fall of it." We have focused on the wise person who pays attention and obeys the words of our Lord, but it is important to remember that God gives people the choice.

It is essential to see clearly that those who would build upon a sandy foundation are heading quickly for trouble. Sand may be attractive and appealing, but it is not durable. A foundation of sand easily erodes at the first heavy rain. This is not the foundation upon which wise builders would seek to erect a lasting house. Frankly, any foundation other than those built upon the Lord Jesus Christ is like the sinking sand.

The question begs to be answered, "Why would anyone not listen to the Lord Jesus and do what His Word commands?" This can be answered by the Lord Jesus Himself as He teaches the parable of the sower, which is recorded for us in Matthew 13:3-9, "And He spoke many things unto them in parables, saying, behold a sower went forth to sow; and when he sowed, some seeds fell by the wayside, and the fowls came and devoured them up. Some fell upon stony places, where they had not much earth, and forthwith they sprung up, because they had no deepness of earth and when the sun was up, they were scorched, and because they had no root they withered away. And some fell among thorns, and the thorns sprung up, and choked them. And other fell into good ground, and brought forth fruit, some an hundredfold, some sixtyfold, some thirtyfold."

The Lord Jesus often spoke in parables. A parable is a story that people would readily understand, but in that story is the application of spiritual truth. The Lord Jesus talked about a very common practice in His time. He spoke of the sowing of seeds which would land upon various types of soil. In His teaching the Lord Jesus was actually speaking about people. The seed is the Word of God, and the soil is the type of human heart which responds in different ways to the seed. The explanation of the parable is found in Matthew 13:18-23, and there we discover that there are four different responses to the Word of God. Let's imagine these four different soils are four different couples who were listening to the Bible being presented.

- ***The couple with the hard hearts*** is described in Matthew 13:19. The Lord Jesus says, "Hear ye therefore the parable of the sower. When anyone hears the word of the kingdom, and understandeth it not, then cometh the wicked one, and catches away that which is sown in his heart. This is he which received seed by the wayside." The first couple listens politely to the Bible being presented; however, their hearts are so hardened that the Scriptures really never penetrate their lives.

  You ask what made their hearts so hardened? It may be difficult to tell for sure, but sometimes people harden their hearts by previously rejecting the Scriptures, living a deepening sinful lifestyle, or simply refusing to listen. This is the couple who is likened to the sower whose seed falls on the trampled path, the hardened wayside. They turn away without bearing any fruit of repentance or eternal life. Does this describe you or your spouse?

- ***The couple with the stony hearts*** is described in Matthew 13:20-21. The illustration continues as the Lord Jesus teaches, "But he who received the seed on stony places, this is he who hears the words and immediately receives it with joy, yet he has no root in himself, but endures only for a while. For when tribulation or persecution arises because of the word, immediately he stumbles." (NKJV)

  This couple is a major disappointment to believers who have high hopes for them. They seem to start off well. They seem to listen to the Bible being presented and immediately respond with great joy and wonderful enthusiasm. But then a little problem arises, and as fast as their enthusiasm exploded, so quickly their turning away takes place. The Scriptures did not take root in their hearts because the Lord said their hearts were stony. There was just enough soil for the seed to appear to be germinating and beginning to grow. Sadly, because there is no deepness of that soil, the plant never takes root properly and will soon wither in the sun. They turn away and bear no productive fruit. Does this describe you or your spouse?

- *The couple with the thorny hearts* is described in Matthew 13:22. Here the Lord Jesus explains, "He also that received seed among the thorns is he that heareth the word, and the cares of this world, and the deceitfulness of riches, choke the word, and he becometh unfruitful." Our third couple also seems to be responding to the Scriptures. This couple hears God's Word, and they seem to be taking it in.

Like the stony-hearted couple, this couple has a great beginning. But it doesn't take long to discover that their hearts are not good for growing a rich productive fruitful crop. They are said to be thorny. What a description.

Think about this carefully. While it may sound obvious, it is still very important to remember that there are at least two miserable things about thorny bushes. First, they hurt! It is painful to deal with a thorny bush because as careful as you can be, sure enough you soon will be scratched and punctured by those jagged thorns. Second, they choke out the nutrients and the rain from reaching the good seed. Who wants to produce a healthy crop of thorns? Right! Whatever beauty or produce that could be grown in that spot is choked out by the thorny growth.

Sure enough, the thorny-hearted couple seems to respond well to the Scriptures, but then the cares of this life, their riches, and the things of this world seem to put a choke hold on them. Probably it won't be as quickly noticeable as the stony heart, but the true nature of this heart will show sooner or later. A struggle rages. The pull of the gospel and the claims of Christ are pulling on one hand, and the cares of this world and their own personal wealth and well-being are pulling on the other hand. Sadly, the cares of this world and their personal situations choke out the good seed of the gospel. Sometimes in spite of good counsel on the temporary state of riches and material substance, the stronghold of substance chokes out the precious gospel that could change their lives. They turn away and bear no lasting fruit. Does this describe you or your spouse?

- ***The couple with the good hearts*** is described in Matthew 13:23. Here the Lord Jesus says, "But he that received seed into the good ground is he that heareth the word, and understandeth it; which also bear fruit, and bring forth, some an hundredfold, some sixty, some thirty."

This is the couple that hears the gospel, and their hearts are tender toward it. The work of the Holy Spirit using the Word of God penetrates. Repentance and acceptance of the gospel is demonstrated by life-changing characteristics. They truly know the Lord Jesus as personal Savior and possess a genuine desire to grow in their spiritual life. Does this describe you or your spouse?

The general teaching of this parable views the first three soils, or hearts, as those belonging to unsaved, unregenerate people. The fourth soil, or heart, belongs to those individuals whose hearts have been changed and now made receptive to the working of the Word in his or her life. The Word of God gets into this heart. It grows. It becomes productive. This person listens to the Word and obeys!

Those who love to garden will quickly see the correlation between the sower, the seed, and the various types of ground. The Word of God is just like the seed. It is living and powerful (Hebrews 4:12). It must be planted and then take root in our hearts (Colossians 3:16). It must be cultivated, which means it must be studied, applied, and practiced (1 Corinthians 3:6-9). It then will bear much fruit (Galatians 5:22-23).

The good soil or the good heart bears the precious desire and even burning passion to love and honor the Lord Jesus. Honestly, this is the very heart and essence of the marriage that grows and stays best friends long after the honeymoon's over.

This is the outworking of lives that are built upon the firm foundation of knowing the Lord Jesus Christ as personal Savior and obeying the Word of God. A good foundation is the absolute key to building a beautiful home as well as building a beautiful marriage. There is no better Foundation to build your marriage upon than the One Who created and established it!

Think about these questions

1. The Lord Jesus spoke about the dangers of anger. Why do you suppose He linked it with murder?

2. Why do you believe that anger is very destructive in marriages?

3. The Lord Jesus spoke about the dangers of adultery. Why do you suppose that He equated lust, which is the desire for that which is forbidden, with adultery, which is the deed of that which is forbidden?

4. Pornography is often said to be harmful to no one else other than the viewer. What is wrong with this statement?

5. The Lord Jesus spoke about divorce and then strongly endorsed the permanence of marriage. Why do you suppose people are so quick to get a divorce today?

6. Imagine that you are a marriage counselor. A couple has told you that they are considering getting a divorce. You want to encourage the couple that this is not the course of action God wants them to take. You want to encourage them that they really can have a good marriage. What are four or five things you would tell them to begin doing immediately to improve their marriage?

7. How is your marriage doing? Are the storms starting to shake your marriage? Is it really built upon the great foundation? Are you the wise couple that has built their marriage upon the Lord?

Before you leave this chapter, it will be very important to honestly consider your heart condition. King David earnestly prayed, "Search me, O God, and know my heart: try me and know my thoughts: And see if there be any wicked way in me, and lead me in the way everlasting" (Psalm 139:23-24).

That was an incredible prayer for this Old Testament man of God. How really special this prayer will be for you to consider as well. Which heart condition best describes yours? Do you and your spouse really know the Lord Jesus as your very own Savior?

Storms

Are you going through stormy times?
Yes, of course, there will be storms.
Those storms rage in their fury, thundering and crashing around us.
The gales cause the best of houses to shake and shutter
as if they seem to be bracing themselves against the fury of the winds
and pelting rains.

But just as surely as the storm comes,
it will also move on.
The storm, as intense as it is, will not last forever.
Storms may howl and beat upon the house,
but they will not last forever.

The storm will cease.
The skies will begin to clear.
The rainbow will appear as rains slowly cease to fall.
The blue sky will return.
The house built upon the firm foundation
may lose a shingle or shutter. But it still stands.

The storm in its fury blew and pounded upon the house.
But it still stands.
The builder was wise and built it
upon the great foundation.

The Lord Jesus Christ spoke these timeless words,
"Whosoever hears these sayings of Mine
and does them,
I will liken him unto a wise man which built his house upon a rock:
And the rain descended, and the floods came,
and the winds blew, and beat upon that house;
and it fell not: for it was founded upon a rock."
Yes, the storm blew.
But the house built on the firm foundation still stands!

Your life is the house. How is your foundation? What a picture of your marriage. Wise couples periodically check for cracks or anything that is potentially damaging to their foundation!

It is my prayer that there will be a little "dust" which is the evidence that you are working in this area in your marriage. Constructing a beautiful marriage is a lot like constructing a beautiful house!

Chapter Five
Decorating and Furnishing

Making Your Home Unique and Special

"Through wisdom is an house builded;
and by understanding it is established:
And by knowledge shall the chambers be filled with all
precious and pleasant riches" (Proverbs 24:3-4)

A house without furnishings is empty.
A house without decorations has an echo.
It screams emptiness.
But when that house is furnished with things
that are significant and beautiful,
then it is amazing to see what happens!
That empty house becomes a beautiful home!

From Grandpa's note: Furnish and decorate it meaningfully, otherwise it will be empty and boring.

Key thought: *There is nothing as exciting as the transformation of a house into a home. 'Character' forms as meaningful decorations are added by the homeowners. The same is true in marriage. Make your marriage beautiful by decorating it with special things that make it unique to you as a couple.*

Ken and Alisha arrived in plenty of time to meet with Henry Mitchell in his office. Their new house was coming along wonderfully. They could hardly believe the changes that had taken place each time they visited the worksite. It was now time to talk with Henry, or Hank as many called him, and make decisions regarding the various cabinets to be installed in the kitchen, the color of the walls, and the tiles and carpeting.

Hank shook hands with the young couple, welcoming them into his office as he said, "Well, that house of yours is coming along nicely. Now it's time for us to make sure that your house becomes the home you want it to be. You have some choices to finalize so that your home will be uniquely yours." Several subcontractors met the young couple along with Henry to make their selections according to their preferences. What a great opportunity this young couple had to turn an empty, echoing house into a beautifully furnished home that would be just right for them!

Likewise, God wants to wonderfully bless your marriage. Don't settle for just simply sharing the same address. Picture your marriage like the home that is under construction, and watch what God can do as you add the special features that only you and your spouse can add to your marriage. The Lord not only desires that your marriage will survive, He wants it to thrive. Great marriages will become great friendships as you and your spouse make your marriage truly unique.

See the Beautiful Design

There is a beautiful correlation between God's awesome act of creation and God's beautiful design of marriage. Think about three key words that are powerful in their richness as they relate to *both* creation and marriage or the home.

Awesome creation

"The LORD by wisdom hath founded the earth; and by understanding hath He established the heavens. By His knowledge the depths are broken up, and the clouds drop down the dew" (Proverbs 3:19-20). Look around and see the handiwork of the Lord God. How awesome is His creation! Though under the Divine curse (Genesis 3:17-19; Romans 8:19-22), His creation is breathtaking in its beauty, intricacies, workings, and design. The galaxy is vast. The molecule is minute. His creation is incredible.

Awesome marriage and home

"Through wisdom is an house builded; and by understanding it is established: and by knowledge shall the chambers be filled with all precious and pleasant riches" (Proverbs 24:3-4).

The Lord marvelously uses the same three words to describe His awesome creation and marriage plans! It will be important to understand these words and apply them in a practical way.

- ***Wisdom*** (*chokmah*) basically means to view the present situation with a discerning eye. Don't misinterpret any situation. By applying this wonderful wisdom to your marriage, you will not act foolishly or carelessly. This special wisdom will help you to conduct yourself in ways that will not create a bad situation. Such discernment is the outflow of comprehending and seeing with clarity.

- ***Understanding*** (*tabuwm*) focuses upon the concept of responding to a situation by using good insight. When you act with good understanding, it will show by the way you respond in word and in action. Unless it is an emergency that requires a quick response, often there is blessing in thinking through the situation in order to respond with insight.

- ***Knowledge*** (*da'ath*) is the wonderful perception that results when wisdom and understanding are combined and blended. This kind of knowledge can also, at times, be used for the word 'skillfulness,' and it gives the idea of quality words and quality actions. One of the greatest joys is to have a growing knowledge of your spouse, your marriage, and what you can do to build a strong and lasting marriage.

Ken and Alisha stood at the worksite of their new house. They were thrilled when the studding was up and the roof was secured. Now their vinyl siding would be applied, and the dry wall was being finished. Finally their house was really beginning to take shape.

Earlier they had met with Henry Mitchell and several of the subcontractors to make the selections that would transform their home to be truly unique to them. How excited they were!

Make It Unique and Beautiful

Likewise, you have the opportunity of making your marriage truly unique and beautiful. As the Lord used wisdom, understanding, and knowledge in the creation of His universe, so the Lord greatly desires for you to ask Him for the wisdom, understanding, and knowledge required to transform your marriage into a thing of beauty!

There are at least five things that couples who exercise this Godly wisdom, practical understanding, and growing knowledge must do to enjoy their unique and beautiful marriage. While this is not a quick "to do" list, these wise courses of action are essential in the building of your marriage.

Love your Lord

What a day it was when the Sadducees were put to silence! Then the Pharisees came to tempt the Lord Jesus. A lawyer spoke up with a question that he thought would put Christ in a hard place to answer. He asked, "Master, which is the great commandment in the law?" (Matthew 22:36).

Foolish lawyer! How impossible it is to entrap the Lord Jesus! How outrageous to think that the Lord Jesus would be confused in talking about the law! He wrote the Law! The lawyer asked his question, and it took no time for the Lord Jesus to reply.

"Thou shalt love the Lord thy God with all thy heart, and with all thy soul, and with all thy mind. This is the first and great commandment" (Matthew 22:37-38). Of all the wonderful commandments, judgments, and statutes of the Lord, to love the Lord your God is the starting point. It is the focal point upon which every other commandment is established. The first requirement to make your marriage beautiful and your friendship lasting is to love the Lord your God.

So, how do you grow in your love for Him? The answer is the same as how you first started to grow in your love for your spouse. You invested time together. You got to know your spouse better. You shared experiences together. You talked and listened to each other. It is the same with the Lord.

The Apostle Paul desired to know the Lord better. He said, "That I may know Him, and the power of His resurrection, and the fellowship of His sufferings, being made conformable unto His death" (Philippians 3:10). The more you get to know Him and the more you share your life with Him, the more you will love Him!

As you and your spouse begin to understand how very much God loves you, you and your spouse will continue to grow in your love for the Lord. God's wonderful love is great (Ephesians 2:4), everlasting (Jeremiah 31:3), and sacrificial (Romans 5:8). When you experience this tremendous love, it likewise manifests itself by loving Him in return.

Couples who really love the Lord seem to demonstrate the following actions.

- *Think* about Him (Matthew 22:42).
- *Trust* Him (Proverbs 3:5-6).
- *Talk* about Him (Psalm 105:2).
- *Take* His ways (Psalm 25:4).
- *Testify* of His goodness and greatness (1 John 4:14-15).
- *Thank* Him often (Psalm 100:4).

Think about these questions

1. Are these characteristics consistently demonstrated in your personal life?

2. Are these characteristics consistently demonstrated in your marriage?

3. What are four or five ways that your love for the Lord is consistently demonstrated in your home and marriage?

4. The Lord Jesus clearly reminds His people, "If you love me, keep my commandments" (John 14:15). What does this verse say to you?

Establish what your core values are and list them

You and your spouse have a really great opportunity to do something very special, if you have never done this, or if it has been a long time since you originally did this. Compile a list together of your top five or ten core values. I say this is special because it is such a rarity. It would seem that some couples never sit down together and establish their core values. For this to take place, you and your spouse must first understand what a value is. Then second, you must talk about what your shared values are, and then last, you need to list these values on paper.

So, what is a core value? To understand what core values are, it will be important to remember that every situation, decision, and viewpoint can be defined by one of three possibilities.

- *The first possibility is your preference.* Your preference has to do with something that is slightly better or more advantageous than other possibilities. Preferences belong in the minor category and usually would be limited to such things as whether you prefer lemon-filled doughnuts to coconut cream, or if you prefer tomato soup over chicken noodle. Preferences change often and may depend on a number of mitigating circumstances.

- *The second possibility is your opinion.* This is a little weightier. There is a little more importance to your opinion than your preference. Typically in the expression of your opinion, you have thought about the situation and perhaps have even prayed about it. You may have taken a little time to research the contributing factors, and as you weighed out various options in your mind, you came to your opinion.

- *The third possibility is your conviction or what you value.* This is the deepest and weightiest among the three possibilities. Your values are what you hold as being critical to life. Your values are based squarely on Scripture or a Scriptural principle. You hold these values as being dear, and you pray that your children will also cherish and treasure them as well.

You can and should develop values or convictions based upon the Word of God. Incredibly, there are Biblical values which relate to every area of marriage, including finances, parenting, intimacy, conflict resolution, marriage-building, decision-making, friendships, and facing difficult situations, to name only a few!

It is sad to think that many couples never talk through what they will adopt as their core values. This does not mean that you must compile a long legalistic list of harsh rules that are hard to live up to. It does mean, however, talking and praying about several core principles that will describe the goals you and your spouse have for your marriage and home.

Have you and your spouse ever compiled such a list of core values?

Decorate your marriage by defining and implementing shared values

You have read about the difference between preferences, opinions and values or convictions. One of the great challenges in every life is to keep these three definitions workable. Sometimes we treat preferences as if they were our values. Other times we treat our values as if they were only preferences. You must learn to define every situation by determining first if it is a matter of preference, opinion, or core value.

Powerful teaching is presented in Deuteronomy 6 which demonstrates how values are implemented. Moses spoke to the second generation of the children of Israel. The first generation had rejected the Lord and despised His ways. They would not enter the Promised Land. The second generation soon would be marching into the new land. Moses pleaded with the people to become a generation with strong and Godly core values.

How does this work?

- *Value conceived.* "Hear O Israel: The LORD our God is one Lord: and thou shalt love the LORD thy God with all thine heart, and with all thy soul, and with all thy might" (6:4-5).

  Core values for believers originate in Who God is and what He means to you. Becoming a man or woman of strong core values takes place over time, as you grow in your love for the LORD your God and your knowledge of Him. This is how values or convictions are conceived. Learn as much as possible throughout your lifetime about the Lord. He is absolutely awesome in every way. Understanding and determining what you believe and what is important to you and your spouse should result because of Who the Lord is.

Read the Word of God daily. Invest time with the Lord, and don't be thinking of everything that you must do while you are praying. View Him as your beloved. As a Christian, the Lord Jesus is your Heavenly fiancé. At any time He may come to take you to His Father's House for the wedding ceremony! Get to know Him as the Love of your life.

Think about these questions

1. Has there been a time that you are certain that you personally asked the Lord Jesus to be your Savior? Do you know Him in this way? If you have doubts, please read the tract "Heaven—Are You Going There?" You'll find it at www.michaelpeck.org. There is help available to you and your spouse, if you don't know the Lord personally.

2. Think back to your Bible reading. What two or three verses have you read in the Bible in the last several weeks that have spoken to your heart and helped you to grow in your knowledge of the Lord?

3. More than a few believers struggle with their prayer life. Many seem to find it easier to read a few verses of Scripture quickly than to invest any time in prayer. Do you struggle with a consistent investment of time in prayer? This does not mean praying for hours. The question begs to be asked, "How is your prayer life? Are you getting to know the Lord better through pryer?"

- ***Values confirmed.*** "And these words, which I command thee this day, shall be in thine heart" (6:6).

God's Word must never be viewed as common or insignificant. Not only must you read the Bible, you must take it to heart. This means that God's Word must be read, believed, applied to daily living, and taught to others who follow you. What a joyous blessing comes to the home of those who love the Lord and take heed to what He says! How precious is the home where husband and wife love the Lord and together honor His Word!

- ***Values communicated.*** "You shall teach them diligently to your children, and shall talk of them when you sit in your house, when you walk by the way, when you lie down, and when you rise up" NKJV (6:7).

This is not the long harsh lecture of out-of-control parents who scream into the faces of their children. Rather, it is the outflow of Godly, gracious, and wise couples who have established the core value of Biblical living in their home. Teaching situations for parents which present themselves as twenty seconds of illustration and application of a life principle based on God's Word are powerful and practical.

The twenty seconds of application quietly but firmly plants the seed of what the situation is, who the Lord is, what the Lord says, and what change needs to take place. This is the inculcation of core values that need to be taught to those who follow us.

- ***Values caught.*** "Now these are the commandments, the statutes, and the judgements, which the LORD your God commanded to teach you, that you might do them in the land whither you go to possess it: That thou mightest fear the LORD thy God, to keep all His statutes, and His commandments, which I command thee, thou, and thy son, and thy son's son, all the days of thy life; and that thy days may be prolonged" (Deuteronomy 6:1-2).

Think of the phrase "you, your son, and your son's son." Moses, in 6:1-2, laid out a plan for teaching children. God had given His Word (6:1) to the husbands and wives as they wandered in the wilderness. They were to fear the Lord, keep His Word, and remember the commandments of the Lord. They were to apply them personally. As they lived them out, their children would follow their pattern, and the grandchildren would follow the same pattern (6:2).

Values probably are more caught than they are taught. Teaching has its place; however, the strongest values by which people live are caught by those who are watching.

Jacqueline came home from her after-school part-time job and seemed unusually quiet. Dad sat down beside and her and asked, "Do you want to talk?"

She looked up and somberly told her dad about a situation at work where one of her co-workers had been arrested. "Not more than fifteen minutes before this, my co-worker had asked me if I wanted some extra cash this week from the register! She assured me that the bosses were not watching and that they weren't even aware of how much should be there.

"I remembered right then a story you told me about when you were a teenager. Remember? You told me that your friends wanted you to do something that was wrong. You said they wanted you to go into a place that would be sinful for you. You knew it was wrong, and you said 'No.' Remember, Dad, how you thought for just a moment. You knew that no one would know you there, and yet you knew it was wrong, and you said, 'No.' Just as the others came out of that place where you would have been if you had joined them, there was your neighbor. I'll never forget that, Dad. You said that not only would your neighbor have known, she would have immediately told your parents and worst of all, the Lord would have known.

"I remembered that happening to you, and I thought for just a second that some extra cash would be wonderful. But I also thought about the Lord, and I thought of you and Mom and how that would hurt you and her. I said, 'No,' because I did not want to hurt the Lord, you and Mom, and even my boss. I knew that it was wrong. I even tried to stop her and warned her that my dad always said, 'It's never right to do wrong no matter what.'

"It might not even have been fifteen minutes later that my boss spoke sternly to my co-worker to come to the office immediately. Two police cars pulled in, and just a couple of minutes later she was taken out in handcuffs!" Jackie said. She softly began to cry. "I'm so glad I said, 'No,' Dad. I just can't tell you how glad I am for how you raised me. You are always reminding me of what the Lord Jesus wants me to do."

That illustrates the inculcation of core values. Sooner or later your children are going to face significant temptation. You probably won't be standing

Decorating and Furnishing 81

beside them. Core values clearly defined, consistently explained, lovingly applied, and wisely rewarded will have lasting blessing for you, your children, and your grandchildren. They decorate your marriage with beauty.

The core values of our home and marriage

While it is not possible for me to present a list of what your values should be, I can share with you what my wife and I have sought to embrace in our personal lives as well as what we have sought to teach our children. Your core values cannot simply be a list that you take from someone else. You must establish *your* core values based upon your own personal decision and dedication to applying them in daily life. For my wife and me, these are several of our core values that have decorated our marriage and home.

- ***We will love the Word of God.*** "O how love I Thy Law! It is my meditation all the day" (Psalm 119:97).

   What a precious statement that must be true in the hearts of every couple that yearns to build a lasting friendship! Such a love for the Word will become your source of strength and guidance. Desiring to read it daily, with so many activities clamoring for your attention, requires discipline.

   Our children still laugh as they remember their mom and dad's rule: "NO BIBLE—NO BREAKFAST! If you don't have time to read the Word of God in the morning, then you don't have time to sit down at the breakfast table for an early meal." Every once in a while, in a loving way, I would meet our children as they arrived for breakfast. They would briefly tell me what portion they had read that morning. I would ask a question or two to see if they understood it, briefly help them to see how to apply it, and then I would welcome them to breakfast.

   Sometimes I would look down the line of faces (we have two biological sons, eight adopted children of three sibling groups, and fifteen foster-parented children), and lo and behold, there would be one of my children ducking out of the line and tearing back to his room. By the time the next to the last gave me their fun report of their Bible reading, that youngster was back in line, beaming from ear to ear!

We didn't want to make it a harsh legalistic commandment and pound Bible reading into our children, but we did want to emphasize its great importance. Today as they teach their children to read God's Word, it is a great blessing to see the love for God's Word being communicated.

- *We will honor the Lord.* "Honor the LORD with thy substance, and with the first-fruits of all thine increase: So shall thy barns be filled with plenty, and thy presses shall burst out with new wine" (Proverbs 3:9-10).

From the time of our engagement until this day, Karen and I have intentionally sought to honor the Lord privately in our hearts, consistently in our home, and honestly in our corporate worship with God's people. Through the years we have seen the importance of seeking to demonstrate our honor for the Lord in our worship (Philippians 2:4-11), Godly living (Titus 2:12), and faith (Hebrews 11:6). We found that as we sought to honor the Lord, we sensed a growing desire to endeavor to be a couple that would be content (Hebrews 13:), diligent (1 Thessalonians 3:17), honest (Romans 13:17), and holy in our lifestyle (1 Peter 1:15-16). Thankfully, this doesn't mean that we have to live perfectly, but as we seek to honor the Lord, it will show in the way we live.

- *We will serve the Lord.* "Serve the LORD with gladness: come before His presence with singing" (Psalm 100:2).

It is important that you and your spouse promise the Lord that you will go anywhere He wants you to go, do anything He wants you to do, and be anything He wants you to be as long as He will go with you. Couples who serve the Lord together discover such a tremendous blessing in the bond between the Lord and each other. Together they get to invest in matters of eternity. How incredibly awesome!

Stop and really consider what your typical week looks like. Are there specific things that you and your spouse are doing to serve the Lord?

Have you ever spoken with your pastor about the opportunities that are available to serve through your local church?

Have you and your spouse been stretched to the point of actually going on a short-term mission's trip? My wife and I had a life-changing experience as we traveled to the Philippines for a several-week ministry. Though we already were serving, that trip gripped our hearts and blessed us incredibly. What's stopping you from serving the Lord in a ministry that He opens to you?

- ***We will try not to grieve the Holy Spirit.*** "And grieve not the Holy Spirit of God, whereby you are sealed unto the day of redemption" (Ephesians 4:30).

You and your spouse must abandon grudges (Ephesians 4:31). In fact, you will not go to bed angry with each other, if you follow God's instructions (Ephesians 4:26). Apologies will come quickly and forgiveness will be extended completely because you have been forgiven much (Ephesians 4:32).

My wife and I tried to be wise parents who consistently helped our children to stop and consider how their actions affected their playmates. When they were unkind, selfish and hurtful, their playmates were saddened. Contrariwise, when they were thoughtful, generous and helpful, their playmates were pleased. Guess what? The same is true for believers and the Holy Spirit. Our actions can either be grievous or a blessing to the precious Holy Spirit. Stop from time to time and consider how your actions as individuals and as the couple affect the Lord.

- ***We will be on guard.*** "Neither give place to the devil" (Ephesians 4:27). You must be very careful not to allow anything to come into your personal lives, your marriage, or your household that would give your spiritual enemy an advantage which would hurt the Lord and your family (Ephesians 4:27). You will erect every safeguard possible to remove those things that would hurt the Lord and give place to the devil.

Carelessness is a disaster waiting to happen! The car ahead was swerving terribly. It sped up and then slowed. It veered from one side of the road to the other. We wondered if the person was having a medical emergency, so I pulled closer. It turns out that the lady was trying to put on her makeup using the rearview mirror as she was driving. Her carelessness could have caused a tragedy.

Fortunately, most people do not drive carelessly like that! But there is another carelessness that is even more dangerous. It is the potential disaster that comes from letting the guard down and giving place or opportunity for the devil to work. Wise believers make it just as difficult as possible for the devil to work in their marriage and home. Just as the windows and doors are locked and double-checked at night to make it more difficult for burglars, safeguards must be set in place ensuring the Lord's blessing. These include Godly choices and convictions in lifestyle, recreation, entertainment, decisions, and conduct.

So how do you erect safeguards in your marriage? How can you live joyfully and still be on guard? Here are the two key things that Karen and I learned to do from the earliest days of our marriage.

We acknowledged that we are redeemed by our great Savior, the Lord Jesus Christ; therefore, it matters how we live in this wicked world. We earnestly tried to be on guard for the things that would dishonor and displease Him. Several Biblical commands greatly affected our lives with the challenge of remembering to Whom we belonged, including Romans 12:1-2, 1 Corinthians 6:18-20, and Ephesians 4:1.

We determined that we are reserved for each other. "My beloved is mine, and I am his" (Song of Solomon 2:16) is a brief statement, and yet it is overflowing with the joy of belonging to one another. Karen and I met in the third grade and grew up together. I can assure you that you don't have to be childhood sweethearts to enjoy the grand blessing of belonging to each other and also, therefore, of reserving yourselves. This prevents fantasizing, flirting, and being inappropriate with another.

These two simple and yet profound challenges from the Word can impact your marriage with a strong and secure safeguard. Your spiritual enemy is real. Don't make it easy for him to harm your marriage.

- ***We will keep eternity in view.*** "Beloved, now are we the sons of God, and it doth not yet appear what we shall be: but we know that when He shall appear, we shall be like Him: for we shall see Him as He is. And every man that hath this hope in him purifieth himself, even as He is pure" (1 John 3:-3).

  Keeping eternity in view is a joyous focus on how short our time is on this earth. Eternity, forever and ever being Home with the Lord and His wonderful family, is a grand and precious truth that should grip the life of every believer. In the homegoing of two of our sons and now as my wife battles cancer, the focus of eternity surely has my attention and affection. You do not have to be in a life crisis to be focused on eternity, however. Keeping the imminent return of our great Savior, the Lord Jesus, ever before us brings about a profound sense of joy and assurance in our personal life as well as our marriage.

  As you live each day looking for the return of the Lord Jesus, focus on the joy that will come when you are Home with Him. Such assurance brings about wonderful blessing. Looking through the grid of eternity brings great help and discernment in viewing the temporary things of life, and it will enrich and strengthen your marriage.

Karen and I did not quickly put together this list of core values with Scripture references. We developed these as the Lord took us on a journey of maturing in our walk and trusting Him in our hearts. Likewise, for your love to grow for the Lord Jesus Christ and for the enduring friendship of your marriage to be enriched, these are the characteristics of Biblical Christianity that God wants to develop in your home and marriage.

Please do not develop your core values based simply on the values of my wife and me. Prayerfully invest time and prayer with your spouse, and in your own words write out *your* core values that best describe your convictions. When you and your spouse have settled on your core values, post them some place where you will both be reminded of their importance and plan to go over them often together.

Celebrate the differences you and your spouse bring to your marriage

You must remember that there are no cookie cutter marriages. Cookie cutters make each cookie identical to the rest of the batch. While you and your spouse must agree upon the core values of your home and marriage, neither the husband nor the wife loses the *personal* identity and personality God has given to them. There are two very different backgrounds, personalities, and perspectives; otherwise the marriage would be boring!

God's wonderful work of making us

"I will praise Thee; for I am fearfully and wonderfully made: marvelous are Thy works; and that my soul knowest right well" (Psalm 139:14). King David made an incredibly interesting statement. He knew far less than we do about conception and development, but just think about the king's statement when he penned the words that we are "fearfully and wonderfully made."

The word "fearfully" is *yare*. This occasionally is used for "terror," but often it is used as "an awesome amazement." King David was absolutely amazed and filled with a sense of awe when he studied the complexity of human beings. He saw how "wonderfully made" His Creator God had designed him to be. He used the word *palah* which gives the idea of "being distinct, being set apart, or being different." God does not mass-produce people on an assembly line. God uses no cookie cutters to make His people.

Rather than allowing differences to be the cause of friction, you can celebrate your differences by seeing how they complement each other. Men and women are very different from each other, but the differences can work well together. Not only are you different physically, you are different in several other ways as well.

You and your spouse process information differently: think of waffles and spaghetti

Our great and awesome Creator God has designed men and women to be incredibly different in several key ways. While we have much in common, we are definitely different. Men and women are very different from each other in the way information is processed. Typically men are best

Decorating and Furnishing

described by the waffle while women are typically best described by spaghetti!

- **The waffle.** A man is very much like the waffle in that he compartmentalizes his approach to most things. Everything is filed in its own little box-like place in his mind. He typically is logical and project-focused. Often he is self-reliant and has a 'conqueror' mentality. It is often difficult for him to stop and ask directions because he is sure he can find it on his own. He usually is not good at multi-tasking because he views one situation at a time in his perspective. This is the way that God has wonderfully made his brain to function.

- **The spaghetti.** A woman is very much like spaghetti in that everything is connected and interwoven. She is much more relational in her perspective and people-focused. Typically asking for help or directions comes very easily for her because she easily connects people, situations, and opportunities. These are usually somehow interwoven. Multi-tasking typically comes easy to her because everything is connected in one way or another. This is the way God has wonderfully made her brain to function.

Does this accurately describe you and your spouse?

Certainly there are exceptions, but typically this is how men and women process information and view situations. Don't let these differences drive a wedge between you and your spouse. Enjoy each other. Try to view things from the perspective of your spouse! Don't assume that your spouse knows what you are thinking. Be clear in how you communicate, and learn to laugh at yourself as well as humorous situations that arise from these differences.

You and your spouse may communicate differently; think of how communication typically takes place

- **Facts.** The man typically focuses on facts. He approaches situations with the desire to fix things and to fix them quickly. Often he is a person of few words and finds it easy to "zone out" when too many words are hurled at him.

- **Feelings.** The woman typically focuses on feelings. She approaches situations with the desire to talk through them. Typically she expresses more words and can be very emotional in expressing them.

Does this accurately describe you and your spouse? In some marriages the exact opposite is true, but typically the facts and feelings statements hold true for men and women. Do you see how this relates to resolving problems and disagreements?

Often men use very few words. By the time he returns home from work he has used up most of his words. On the other hand, his wife is eager to see him in the evening, and she has many more words yet to speak. He wants quietness; she wants to share. When there is a misunderstanding, he simply wants to fix it as quickly as possible. She wants to talk through the situation and explain her feelings.

- **Bridges and connections.** Be careful never to allow these differences in communication to build a wall between you and your spouse! Communication is much like a bridge that connects two important bodies of land. When you and your spouse communicate well, you are building a beautiful bridge that connects you in a very special and meaningful bond. Much like the emerging beauty of a house as construction takes place, a marriage is beautified as joy, love, trust, and devotion are expressed through good communication.

The Apostle Paul provided very good counsel for the church at Ephesus. He told them "But speaking the truth in love, may grow up into Him in all things, which is the head, even Christ" (Ephesians 4:15). This is a powerful verse to describe good communication.

Think of the necessary ingredients for good communication in marriage. Husbands and wives must talk to each other. They must be honest. In their honesty they must be intentional to wrap the truth in loving words and deeds! Together they must enjoy the growing and maturing process. Ultimately they desire to please and glorify the Lord Jesus with their communication.

Decorating and Furnishing

Think about these questions

1. Think about the statements about facts and feelings. Do these accurately represent your marriage?

2. Think about how you and your spouse are communicating with each other. Do you or your spouse think there is room for improvement in this? If so, in what ways?

What beauty and blessings result when couples communicate Biblically. Bridges are built. Connections are reinforced. Friendship builds long after the honeymoon's over.

You and your spouse may view intimacy differently

- *Sight!* Men typically are highly stimulated by sight and much quicker to spring into action sexually. More than one wife has been amazed that her husband could be so ready to initiate sexual activity. Men typically are quick to respond to the suggestion of the act of intimacy and are more quickly aroused.

- *Feelings!* Ladies are typically stimulated by feelings, by the touch, by the loving words, and romantic actions that take place over a longer period of time. Usually the wife doesn't initiate sexual intimacy as often as does her husband. However, when she does it is usually a wonderful blessing to her husband. For the typical lady, intimacy is not nearly as spontaneous. It is often planned and reinforced by the words and actions of her husband demonstrating that he cherishes her. Intimacy is the situation from which the actual sexual act flows, so she is slower to respond and needs time to become aroused.

Does this sound like it accurately describes you and your spouse? While there certainly are exceptions to this rule, this is the typical difference between how men and women view sexual intimacy. Don't allow your differences to become obstacles.

Each husband needs to understand that this is the way the Creator God has designed his wife. She is to be cherished, and the relationship you enjoy with her as her husband is to be nurtured. On the other hand, wives, do not miss the joy of sexual intimacy simply because you are not in the "mood." Understand the needs of your husband, and be thrilled that he finds you desirous. Seek to find unique ways of handling the differences in how you view sexual intimacy.

Some couples develop a little game that indicates that either he or she is "interested in sexual intimacy." Sometimes it is a certain cup that will be brought out from the cupboard and placed in an obvious setting that is a cute way of saying, "I am interested! How about you?" Some couples have a special little piece of paper with an exclamation point on it. This is placed in a conspicuous setting, and it brings up the possibility of intimacy in a cute and creative way.

Don't allow the differences in how you and your spouse view intimacy to become a point of frustration to you. As in the decorating of a beautiful home, let the joy of sexual intimacy be fresh, flirtatious, and fulfilling. Share this with no one other than your spouse. Remember what the writer of Hebrews states, "Marriage is honorable in all, and the bed undefiled" (Hebrews 13:4). Sexual relations between the husband and his wife is a beautiful gift. It is not to be withheld as punishment nor is it to be given as reward. Paul's counsel to the church at Corinth is outstanding as found in I Corinthians 7:3-5 (NKJV) where he said, "Let the husband render to his wife the affection due her, and likewise also the wife to her husband. The wife does not have the authority over her own body, but the husband does. And likewise the husband does not have authority over his own body, but the wife does. Do not deprive one another except with consent for a time, that you may give yourselves to fasting and prayers; and come together again so that Satan does not tempt you because of your lack of self-control."

Even if the situation should arise where a medical condition makes the sexual act impossible, it is still possible to have an intimate relationship. Creative husbands and wives have found that closeness can be developed and expressed in an exciting manner, even if sexual intercourse is not possible. Ask the Lord to help you to be the kind of spouse that wants to create an intimate and loving situation to be shared with your spouse, exclusively, and for a lifetime.

Think about these questions

1. In what ways are you very similar to your spouse?

2. In what ways are you different from your spouse?

3. How would you honestly describe the differences you and your spouse bring to your marriage? Do you view these as bridges that draw you closer or walls that push you apart?

   - What are some of the bridges the draw you closer?
   - What are some of the walls the push you apart?

How you and your spouse demonstrate respect and priority

"Submitting yourselves one to another in the fear of God" (Ephesians 5:21).

Respect is that sense of understanding the great worth, importance, or significance of something or someone. Priority is respect in action. When you have such respect for your spouse, it is demonstrated by giving him or her priority in your attitude, thoughts, words, and actions.

Most husbands have the portion of the Ephesians 5 passage memorized wherein Paul tells the wife to be in submission to her own husband (5:22). Most wives have the portion of Ephesians 5 memorized that tells the husband to love his wife as Christ loved the church and gave Himself for her (5:25). However, sometimes husbands and wives forget that the basis for a beautiful marriage is found in *mutual submission,* which is rooted in the fear of God (5:21).

The word "submitting" is *hypotasso,* which has to do with "arranging under, yielding to one another." It is the same word that will be found one verse later commanding wives to submit to their own husbands. It's pretty startling to some husbands to discover that God not only commands the wife to submit to him but He also commands him to be in submission to her!

The idea of "fear" is *phobos,* which has two different meanings. First, it means "to be in dread, or that which strikes terror." The second meaning of the word is that which results in "a sense of profound awe or reverence."

Beautiful marriages begin with a husband and wife having an abiding sense of awe and reverence for God. They have a good old-fashioned healthy sense of terror at the thought of the holiness and power of the Lord God Almighty. From this reverence for God flows a beautiful and healthy respect and priority for each other.

Ken and Alisha were so excited. They had chosen the cabinetry, the carpets, the tiling, and the colors of the walls. These things would make their house beautiful and unique to them. They would also learn that their marriage could be built into a blessed and beautiful relationship, if they would grow in their respect and priority for one another.

Demonstrating respect for your spouse. How do you demonstrate respect for your spouse? The answer begins with appreciating God's grace and asking for His help. Make the commitment to Him and your spouse to demonstrate respect for the position he or she holds. This will be true even if you cannot respect your spouse's actions. This will not come automatically. You must be intentional and consistent. Here are some suggestions as to how to communicate respect.

- You must be careful to express with your words and actions how much your mate means to you.
- You must seek to be sensitive to your spouse's situation, feelings, and desires.
- You must be careful about the tone of your voice and the choice of your words.
- You must be careful to consult with your spouse about the decisions that need to be made.
- You must recognize the strength of your spouse and appreciate those strengths.
- You must accept the weaknesses of your spouse as you pray for your mate and seek to be an encouragement.
- You must be careful about the way you fool with your spouse, especially when you are out in public.
- You must demonstrate proper respect for your spouse's family. Even if you disagree with the way that your in-laws live, they are the mother and father of your spouse, and that position they hold is one that must be respected.

Decorating and Furnishing

- You must begin the day communicating your love and conclude the day in the same way. Be careful in the routine that your marriage does not become routine! Make time for affection, hugs, and kisses. You must seek to become gentle and gracious as you seek the well-being of your spouse.

Respect is not writing out a list and checking it off. Respect is the character quality of a life that reverences the Lord God Almighty and cherishes one's spouse.

Demonstrating priority. Next to the Lord, your spouse and your marriage must be the highest priority in your life. Your spouse needs to have the assurance of being a special priority in your life. Read these few gentle hints for demonstrating to your spouse that you are making him or her and your marriage the highest priority.

- Guard your marriage. Do nothing that would cause your spouse to distrust you. Live in such a way that your spouse can easily see that you are serious about your relationship and faithfulness.
- Seek to make special days *really* special! Whatever days--birthdays, anniversaries of special days, or days that celebrate something important to your spouse should be made very special.
- Continue to date and invest yourself in the life of your spouse. Date regularly. Do special things, such as writing a note, purchasing a gift, making a phone call or sending an email just to let your spouse know that he or she is on your mind.
- Communicate with your spouse, but do not interrupt. Don't be sitting on the edge of your seat waiting for your spouse to stop talking. Listen. Be quiet. Don't be thinking ahead about how you are going to answer your spouse. Be a good communicator. Look at your spouse when he or she is speaking. Give your spouse your full attention. Focus on your spouse.
- Encourage your spouse. What can you do to be an encouragement? Remember that you are not responsible to change your spouse. Don't be constantly pointing out weaknesses. Look for those things for which you are thankful and share them with your spouse.
- Intimacy is not just sexuality. Sex is part of intimacy, but intimacy is much more than this. Intimacy is the growing together and closeness

that comes between a husband and wife. It is nurtured by respect, trust, hugs, touches, and words.
- Admit when you are wrong. Don't make excuses. Genuinely ask for forgiveness, and do not continue the offending practice.
- Forgive quickly when offenses come along. Never carry a grudge or become bitter. Rather, be quick in helping to resolve conflicts.
- Ask the Lord to give you wisdom as to how to demonstrate the priority of your marriage. Pray often for the strength to protect your marriage from sin or failure.

Do these things describe your consistent actions?

There is a danger in becoming overwhelmed with the daily schedule. It will be very easy for you to slide into a hectic routine, especially if you are a very busy person. The danger of a hectic routine is that marriage requires intentional investment of time and yourself. When you get too busy, unfortunate things can occur. Important things slide. Priorities shift. Couples drift apart and eventually come to the place where they must acknowledge that they are nearly strangers. Do not live as a stranger with your spouse! Who would ever want to live that way? Demonstrating respect and priority will draw you closer and beautify your marriage and home.

How you and your spouse make special memories

"Beware that thou forget not the Lord thy God, in not keeping His commandments, and His judgments, and His statutes which I command thee this day" (Deuteronomy 8:11). God warns that there is an ever-present danger that resides in every human being, and that is forgetfulness. Human beings are forgetful folks.

The word "remember" occurs 148 times in 144 verses in the King James Version of the Bible. Because humans are prone to forget, God sends special reminders. After defeating the Amalekites, Moses commanded, "Write this for a memorial in a book, and rehearse it in the ears of Joshua: for I will utterly put out the remembrance of Amalek from under Heaven" (Exodus 17:14). This memorial book was to help Joshua remember the way to victory.

Later, as Joshua led the second generation across the flooded Jordan River, he not only set up memorial stones in the middle of the river, he commanded the men to carry memorial stones up and out of the waters. He used these stones to build a memorial in a conspicuous place. Later generations would see the memorial stones and remember how God had led His children through the flooded river to bring them to the Promised Land (Joshua 4:8).

Wise couples break out of the doldrums and boring routines to make special memories together. These memories are precious reminders of the faithfulness of God, the joyfulness of being connected in marriage, and the many ways that the Lord has walked along with them through the journey of a lifetime. Does this describe you and your spouse?

- Do you ever watch the sunset while holding the hand of your spouse?
- Do you ever just snuggle on the couch in front of the fireplace?
- Do you ever observe and celebrate the special occasions of life?
- Do you ever share secrets together? How long ago was the last time?
- Do you have things that are special to you and known only to you and your spouse?
- Do you ever record the special ways God has blessed your marriage and home?
- What are you doing to make memories in your marriage?

It was a cloudy day when Henry Mitchell and his brothers, Aaron and Sam, stood with Ken and Alisha in the driveway of their newly completed house. It looked like rain could come at any moment, but the weather didn't matter. Nothing could damper their spirits. They would never forget this day.

Their brand-new house was finished. It would take just a little time to take the final walk through, and then would come the brief ceremony that the Mitchell brothers always did in handing over the keys to the new owners. Their new house, constructed perfectly for their budget, certainly fulfilled their expectations. It was built upon a great foundation. The blueprint was followed fully. Every room reflected the quality care and building of the Mitchell and Sons builders. Ken and Alisha were eager to furnish, fashion, and decorate it just the way they wanted it.

Ken said to them, "We absolutely love this house. We have thought a lot about what you told us, Mr. Mitchell, at the beginning of the building project. We want you to know that we truly do appreciate your wonderful construction and your counsel to build our marriage upon the Lord Jesus, just as wisely as you have built our house."

With that, Henry Mitchell led the little group in prayer and asked God to bless Ken and Alisha. He then presented them with their keys and a beautiful plaque that would be seen by Ken and Alisha through the years. It read,

**Ken and Alisha's house
was built by Mitchell and Sons Construction
but
Ken and Alisha's home
is being built by the Lord Jesus Christ,
the Master Designer!**

Think about these questions

1. Do you have a marriage that is based on wisdom, understanding, and knowledge? If so, what are some of the ways you and your spouse demonstrate this?

    If you cannot think of any ways that this wisdom, understanding, and knowledge are expressed, what are several specific things that you are willing to do to change this?

2. What are two or three things that you routinely do to communicate respect and priority to your spouse?

3. How does your spouse communicate respect and priority to you?

4. Have you and your spouse thought through and compiled a list of core values? If not, what is keeping you from doing this?

5. How do you regularly communicate and demonstrate to your spouse that he or she is loved and cherished?

Turning it Into Beauty

The empty house echoes.
The bare walls are stark and lonely.
The cement slab is cold and uninviting.
Then the carpeting and the tiling are installed.
The painters arrive with their buckets of the perfect colors
selected by my spouse and me.
The furniture arrives and is placed just where we want it to be.
The decorations and the furnishings are special to us,
and as we arrange them, they seem just right to us.
The pictures are mounted on the wall.
The clock is hung above the mantle.
The antique furnishings from our grandparents' home
are displayed strategically.
The greenery of our plants brings life itself to our rooms.
This is no longer an empty *house*;
it is now our beautiful *home*.
It's decorated and furnished just the way we want it.
Similarly, our marriage must become much more
than a cold, barren, and empty relationship.
Through intentional obedience to the Word of God,
a marriage of beauty begins to unfold.
God wants to create
and establish a beautiful marriage for you!
He Who makes the incredible sunset
is the same One that can
make marriage uniquely beautiful.

It is my prayer that there will be a little "dust" which is the evidence that you are working in this area of your marriage. Constructing a beautiful marriage is a lot like constructing a beautiful home!

Chapter Six
Watching for Anything Harmful

Big Storms, Bad Thieves, and Little Bugs

"Finally, my brethren, be strong in the Lord, and in the power of His might. Put on the whole armor of God, that ye may be able to stand against the wiles of the devil. For we wrestle not against flesh and blood, but against principalities, against powers, against the rulers of the darkness of this world, against spiritual wickedness in high places. Wherefore take unto you the whole armor of God, that ye may be able to withstand in the evil day, and having done all, to stand. Stand therefore"
(Ephesians 6:10-14a).

Learning to be diligent is crucial.
Every house is susceptible to potential dangers.
Pretending nothing will ever happen does not help.
It is the same way in marriage.
The potential dangers for houses and marriages are very similar.
Be diligent.
This is no time for a foolish and wishful false sense of security.
Know the potential enemies.
Remember that some of the most destructive enemies appear to be innocent and harmless.
Learn how to spot them.
Learn how to overcome them.

From Grandpa's note: Secure your home and make it safe. Danger comes from big storms, bad thieves, and little bugs!

Key thought: *Living in denial of potential danger is a horrible mistake. A recent flood insurance commercial shows a couple sitting in their living room. They are going about their typical business as flood waters begin to rise. Neither admits to a problem until the dog floats out the front door! Better to admit and fix the problem while it is little. It will become bigger!*

After presenting Ken and Alisha their keys and the wall plaque from Mitchell and Sons Construction, Henry Mitchell said to the young couple, "Now folks, I want you to give serious thought to getting the tornado warning system from the National Weather Service, as well as a home security system. We don't want any tornadoes roaring up on you, nor do we want any thieves sneaking up either.

"I don't want to scare you. Well, maybe I do, just a little. I really do want you to be on guard and secure. There's one more thing for which you need to be on guard. Know what it is? Termites! Those are miserable little pests that are around in this area. Be on guard, and keep on top of the situation." Henry explained how to prevent them. With that he gave the couple a hug and walked to his truck.

It's hard to describe Ken and Alisha's excitement. Finally! Their new house was furnished and decorated! Neither Ken nor Alisha was extravagant in their preferences. Even though many of the items they found were on sale, their house was beautifully decorated just the way they wanted it to be.

When the teacher of their Sunday school class asked for a volunteer to host the next class outing, Ken and Alisha looked at each other, smiled and immediately volunteered! They would be delighted to have the class come to their new home. Not that they wanted to show it off with a wrong sense of pride; they were just so thrilled with the wonderful way the Lord had provided for them that they wanted to share with others and make their home available.

One of the first couples to arrive at the cookout hosted by Ken and Alisha was Paul and Alexandra. As the ladies chatted in the kitchen, Ken and Paul stepped out on the deck because it was just about time to start the gas grill. Paul and Alexandra were new to the group, and this would be the first time that they would be involved in a social gathering with other couples from their new church.

"Well, Paul, I am so happy that you and your dear wife have started attending our church. We are thrilled that the Lord brought you folks to us, and we trust that we will be a blessing to you," Ken said as he lowered the lid on the heating gas grill. He continued, "This is the first chance I've had to really get to know you and your wife a little better. I hope that you will feel right at home and will enjoy the evening with the rest of the class."

Paul smiled and replied, "Well, thanks for having us tonight, Ken. I really love your new home. It is absolutely beautiful. How long have you been in it?"

"Let's see, we have actually been in our home for about three months. I can't believe how fast time is going!" Ken replied. "We still have a little more work to do. I hope no one is planning to stay overnight because we still do not have the guest room furnished!" Ken said laughingly.

"Oh, no!" Paul teased. "I absolutely was planning to stay overnight tonight. I guess I have to sleep on the floor." Both men laughed. "Seriously, your home is lovely, and I really liked the plaque that I saw on the way in. It said something about 'Mitchell and Sons built this house but only the Lord can build the home,' or something like that," Paul said.

"Yes, that's our special plaque. It was presented to us by the builders. It actually says, 'Ken and Alisha's house was built by Mitchell and Sons Construction, but Ken and Alisha's home is being built by the Lord Jesus Christ, the Master Designer!' We really want this to be the theme motto of our home and married life," Ken said.

The men enjoyed their conversation together out by the grilling meat before the other couples arrived. Throughout the course of the conversation, Ken eventually asked about Paul's occupation.

"I own a home security business!" Paul replied. "Actually, my company covers any kind of potential dangers to a person's home. We professionally clean and repair damage caused by storms. Our company has a department that installs home security devices against intruders. We even have a division that protects against pests," Paul said. "I probably sound like I am doing a commercial, but we do most of the typical types of pest control. Most of my business deals with termites. Believe me, they're little and silent, but they are sinister. You'll want to be on guard for them, Ken," Paul said with a note of caution in his voice.

Ken looked up from the grill and replied, "Storm damage, home invasion, and destructive pests sound like they must keep you pretty busy, Paul. You won't believe it, but our builders spoke with us about similar things. I would say that maybe the Lord is trying to get my attention on this matter!" Ken said thoughtfully.

The evening with the other couples from church was a huge blessing to Ken and Alisha. Afterwards Ken was sharing with his wife about Paul's occupation and how he had covered the very things Henry Mitchell had warned them about.

"We are prepared for the storms with the best insurance possible. We have a great security system to protect our home against an invasion, but I think I need to talk to Paul about termites. The last thing we want to ever happen is to have termites invade us. Even though Mr. Mitchell told us the signs, I'm not totally confident that I know what to be watching for. They are so little, but they create such huge problems," Ken said with certainty.

"Storms, invaders, and termites," Alisha shuttered to even speak about them. "I know we need to be protected as best as possible."

"Yeah," Ken said as he hugged his wife, "I know they are real potential problems, but you know what? Alisha, I was thinking about how these things could be compared to potential dangers in our marriage. I want to be on guard for all of those as well," Ken told his wife as they headed to the kitchen to clean up from the class party.

It was a great night in their lives.

The Certainty of Storms

The National Weather Service radio blared out the message, "Severe thunderstorm warning is in effect in our area for the next two hours. Expect dangerous lightning, large hail and strong winds. Take shelter immediately."

That message went out to an area population of thousands. Amazingly, there were two types of responses to such a warning. Foolish people ignored it and acted as if no storm would ever come into their area. Hence, they took no precautions and suffered the consequences for their actions. Wise people heeded the storm warning and took proper precautions.

As you read the Bible, you will discover some literal, actual storms thundering upon the earth. More often, the Scriptures demonstrate that people are caught up from time to time in difficult situations that can best be described figuratively as a storm! Job certainly felt that way. In anguish he listened to his so-called 'friend,' Eliphaz, who made the declaration, "Man is born unto trouble as the sparks fly upward" (Job 5:7).

You know from your own experience that there are two kinds of stormy situations.

The storms of life Peter wrote about

Life is hard. Problems abound at times. There are two kinds of problems or storms that can come. Think about the times these storms have come into your life.

- *The storm you brought on yourself.* This storm is so painful. It is unnecessary and often could have been avoided. You and probably most folks that you know have experienced this "storm." It is the stormy consequences of your wrong choices, choices that were unwise and disobedient to the Lord. You have experienced the unwanted and unhappy consequences of such actions. It is a "storm" that has bitter regrets.

    Peter gives a strong warning about this in his Epistle when he writes, "But let none of you suffer as a murderer, or as a thief, or as an evildoer, or as a busybody in other men's matters" (1 Peter 4:15).

    Sinful choices and stormy trials are part of life. Sin changed everything when it entered God's perfect created world. Even after you confess your sin, there are still consequences of wrong choices which are allowed by an infinitely wise and loving Father to discipline and bring you into a closer walk with Him. He wants to reveal His power and glory, and ultimately make you more like your Savior.

- ***The storm you didn't bring on yourself.*** Peter also speaks of this kind of storm or trial in the same passage, "Yet if any man suffer as a Christian, let him not be ashamed; but let him glorify God on this behalf" (1 Peter 4:17). It would be wonderful if you would take a few minutes and read the entire passage of 1 Peter 4:1-19. There you will discover the many principles that God wants to bring into your marriage, especially in the stormy times.

In the next few pages you will read about two different couples. In the case of Marty and Jeannine, see how his actions brought consequences that hurt not only himself but his wife as well. The second couple experienced quite a trial through no fault of their own. Watch for the lessons to be learned from both couples. Are there any similarities in your marriage to either couple?

Think of Marty and Jeannine and the storm he brought on himself

Marty brought much heartache into his life and marriage. Though his wife Jeannine prayed and occasionally would plead with her husband, he didn't stop his drinking. "I can stop whenever I want," an arrogant Marty shouted. "I don't need you to tell me anything!" he said as he stormed out of the house, slamming the door behind him.

Less than fifteen minutes later, he was stopped by the state police for driving while intoxicated. Since this was not his first offense, Marty lost his driver's license as well as his job. In a time of sobriety, he held his head in his hands and sobbed. "What have I done, Jeannine? What have I done?" This was a storm that was very much avoidable. Others would suffer in this stormy trial because of Marty's sinful choices.

How great is the hurt when unnecessary storms arise. Many homes exist today in unnecessary and stormy exchanges, complete with dramatic lightning-like strikes of hurtful words, angry responses, and sinful actions.

A man in the Bible named Nabal is a good illustration of such an avoidable storm. His name means "fool." Read about his foolish life and actions that brought a storm upon himself and his family in 1 Samuel 25:4-38.

1. What brought on the storm in Nabal's life?

2. How does his precious wife Abigail suffer needlessly because of Nabal's actions?

3. Describe the last days of Nabal's life. How is his suffering brought on as a result of his sinful actions?

Think again of the Apostle Peter's writing about such storms. He said, "But let none of you suffer as a murderer, or as a thief, or as an evildoer, or as a busybody in other men's matters" (1 Peter 4:14). What great counsel and direction! Don't live sinfully or carelessly. Such living guarantees an unwanted and unnecessary storm.

4. How could Nabal's life have been lived differently?

5. Take a moment to read Proverbs 6:12-15. In what way does such a person bring trouble upon himself?

6. Think about your own marriage. Can you think of times that your actions brought an unnecessary storm of difficulty? If so, have you ever resolved this with your spouse and others who have been hurt?

Helps for dealing with the avoidable storms

What if you sinned and now the consequences are bitter? The avoidable storm has been brought on by your sinful choice or an unwise action. What do you now? What steps do you need to take in this kind of storm? Please do not view this as a quick list for fast fixes. Think through these areas carefully.

- Ask the Lord to give you wisdom (James 1:5).
- If you are aware of your sinful actions, then confess them to the Lord (1John 1:9).
- If your sinful actions have hurt others, take the initiative in acknowledging your actions and ask for forgiveness (Luke 15:18-20a).
- Put off the sinful action and put on appropriate living (Ephesians 5:22-24). The Apostle Paul indicated that sinful living is inappropriate for the believer. The Lord wants to strengthen His people to be overcomers and to put off sinful living just as soiled, dirty clothing is removed at the end of the day. Likewise, appropriate life actions are to replace the sinful actions. Picture putting on the new actions as

you would put on new or clean clothes. As you read the Scriptures and invest time in prayer, you will discover a new and growing desire to live Biblically.
- Avoid unnecessary storms by understanding the law of sowing and reaping (Galatians 6:7). There will be consequences for your actions in both the negative and positive sense.
- Treat others the way you would like to be treated (Matthew 7:12). Think of how this relates to your spouse and your marriage. Never take your spouse for granted. Treat your spouse in such a way that not only will the Lord be pleased but your spouse will be blessed as well.

Not all trials are consequences of our sinful choices. Occasionally there will be unavoidable stormy situations that are not brought on by any sinful or foolish action of you or your spouse. At times, your life can face a sudden trial. In fact, you might be going through a series of heavy trials right now. What do you do?

The Lord Jesus spoke of such trials as He Himself was going through the most difficult days imaginable. On the night before He died on the cross He said, "In the world, ye shall have tribulation" (John 16:33). Job confirmed this when he declared, "Man that is of few days and full of trouble" (Job 14:1).

Think of Luke and Sarah and the storm they didn't bring on themselves

Luke and Sarah are such an example of the stormy trial over which they had no control. They were so excited about the pregnancy. They both had dreamed of the day that they would be able to hold their little baby in their arms. Knowing that their baby was a boy, they had started looking through the lists of boys' names. Finally they had decided on the name 'Jeffrey Michael.'

As the due date approached, they grew with anticipation of the birth of little Jeffrey. The morning came that labor began. Everything appeared normal until Jeffrey arrived in the world. He was quickly swept from the birthing center of the hospital and rushed by ambulance to the Neonatal Intensive Care Unit in a distant hospital.

Finally the doctor came to the frightened couple to speak with them. He somberly said, "Your child has very serious heart problems. I cannot guarantee that he is going to live. And if he does, he will need many surgeries."

Luke and Sarah didn't cause this trial. They didn't do anything to bring this dreadfully stormy time into their lives, but they knew that God had a perfect plan. Their entire family walked with the Lord and grew closer together through the four years that God gave them with their Jeffrey Michael. The lessons learned, the strength received, and the blessings that came would be tremendous.

Perhaps you, your spouse and family have walked through such a stormy trial. Most couples walk through storms that are less intense and happier in outcomes.

As devastating as these situations are at the time, the lessons gleaned from them must never be wasted. They are allowed of the Lord to come into your married life. Think back over some of the unavoidable storms you and your spouse have faced or that your friends might be facing right now. Can you relate to any of these things?

- The death of a loved one
- The loss of employment
- An illness that comes into the life of your spouse or child which is much more difficult than the illness that comes into your own life
- A sudden injury that changes everything, at least for a while
- A major disappointment
- A misunderstanding held by an offended friend that weighs heavily upon you
- The "check engine light" on the dashboard of your car
- A friend moves away
- The downsizing at work resulting in more responsibilities at the same pay level
- Your friends have gotten pregnant, but you and your spouse cannot seem to conceive
- A time of uncertainly where you do not know how a situation will be resolved causes you to worry even though you know you shouldn't

- A significant decision such as your company wants you to move across the country and your continued employment depends on your willingness to move

Helps for you and your spouse to survive and thrive in those unavoidable storms

Though you have not brought the storm or trial upon yourself, there are several really important things to think through when the unavoidable storm hits you and your family. Don't let the trial push you and your spouse apart. Come together and connect in an intentional, compassionate, embracing way in your marriage. Invest extra energy and attention on each other. Are you moving toward or away from your spouse?

Job is a great illustration of a person experiencing the unavoidable storm. His situation was actually more like a hurricane.

1. How did Job live, according to Job 1:1?

2. What losses did Job experience in this terrible stormy trial, according to Job 1:19?

3. How did Job express his sorrow, according to Job 1:20?

4. How did Job speak to the Lord during his trial, according to Job 1:21-22?

Job was not an unfeeling, unemotional robot. He was overwhelmed with the horrific news that within a few hours he had lost his entire business. Suddenly those news reports paled in comparison to the news that his children, all of his children, had been killed in a building collapse. In the dust of the earth Job's sorrow is expressed. Two really significant things take place in the life of the grief-stricken patriarch.

- ***He continued to worship God*** (Job 1:20). Notice how Job was worshipping before the trial took place (Job 1:5). Read again how Job worshipped *in* the trial. This is a major principle to be grasped. If you worship God in the good times, be sure that your worship of Him continues in the hard times. If He truly is worthy of your worship in times of good, plenty, and blessing, then your great Lord God is worthy of your worship in times of trial, hardship, and sorrow.

- ***He controlled what he said.*** Job refrained from spouting off in anger and saying things he would later regret (Job 1:21-22). Restraint is such a wise choice when the storm is raging. Understand that restraint does not mean that you clam up, refuse to acknowledge it and deny that it is happening. Being able to talk about your situation is really important.

  This restraint encourages you to speak honestly of the grief and hurt that you are feeling but to refrain from saying things in anger that dishonor the Lord. This is not easy. It wasn't for Job. It won't be for you. But when the storm has passed, you'll be glad that you not only worshipped but that you guarded your words as well.

  Sometimes after the onset of the trial when a spouse has said regrettable things, significant hurt takes place that wounds emotionally. If this has happened to you, in order for friendship to endure long after the honeymoon's over, you will need to wisely rebuild with confession, forgiveness and restoration.

What wonderful blessing results when fears are honestly expressed and quiet trust in the Lord and in His plan takes place. That's what happened with Luke and Sarah. As filled with fear as this young couple was, they were committed to recognizing the worthiness of their great God in the time of trial. Though their hearts were breaking as their young child struggled to live, they guarded their hearts, attitudes, and words. They didn't understand why the Lord had allowed this to happen, but they were convinced that God could be trusted with their little boy. They never charged God with being unfair and unkind. They didn't grow angry and resentful. They worshipped and guarded their words.

No doubt it will be much easier for you to praise the Lord when things are going well. It's awesome, though, to acknowledge your genuine sorrow in the storm while maintaining your precious worship. Guarding your words is really a matter of guarding your heart. This is especially true during the stormy trials that are sure to come.

You'll be wise to anticipate the storms and prepare for them

Wise homeowners live with the probability of storms and, therefore, make provision for those times. Families who live in a tornado alley have a storm cellar. Homeowners living near the Great Lakes have snow removal equipment. Likewise, there are things you and your spouse can do in anticipation of stormy trials.

> • *The Lordship of Christ.* Really settle the question of who is in charge of your life and marriage. Think of what the Lord Jesus said, "You call me Master and Lord: and you say well; for so I am" (John 13:13). He poses a tremendous question when he asked, "And why call you me Lord, Lord, and do not the things which I say?" (Luke 6:46).

When Christ is the Lord of your life, the biggest question relating to Who is in charge is answered. Many couples wrestle with this question. It is a matter of great concern when couples live their lives as if they will never be accountable to the Lord Jesus. Little thought is given to Him. Little time is devoted to Him. Little interest is directed toward Him. What place does the Lord Jesus have in your life and marriage?

Are you and your spouse devoted followers of Jesus Christ, the Lord of life?

Think about these questions

1. What did the Lord Jesus tell His disciples to do in Matthew 11:28-30?

2. What does the Lord's teaching of the 'taking of the yoke and learning from Him' mean to you?

Be assured that the Lord Jesus will allow things to enter your marriage that you probably would not choose. He will take you down roads that you would rather avoid, but you can count on the fact that He is too wise to make any mistakes. His ways are always best. Take a few moments to read God's response from the whirlwind to Job (Job 38:1- 41:34). He is the sovereign God. His plan can be trusted. His ways are perfect.

When you and your spouse are both walking with the Lord, there will be a bond that can best be strengthened in the time of a stormy trial. You will be able to pray together and encourage one another as you go through the trial together.

- *Face the stormy trial but not in your own strength.* Don't face the trial in your own strength. Perhaps you are a fixer! You can find ways to fix almost everything. While there may be things that the Lord wants you to do, facing the trial in your own strength is not one of them.

  King David himself provides good counsel for you and your spouse, if you are going through a difficult trial. He said, "From the end of the earth will I cry unto Thee, when my heart is overwhelmed: lead me to the rock that is higher than I. For Thou hast been a shelter for me from the enemy" (Psalm 61:2-3).

  Several Psalms later King David wrote, "O God, Thou are my God; early will I seek Thee: my soul thirsteth for Thee" (Psalm 63:1). The Lord never wants His children to face the hard times alone. He wants you and your spouse to know the strength that comes by seeking Him together. What wonderful blessings will result from you and your spouse holding hands, praying together, praying for each other, and seeking the Lord, as David said, "early"!

  Seek Him early in your marriage. Seek Him early in the trial. Seek Him early in the day. Come to discover His amazing lovingkindness (Psalm 63:3) and determine to follow Him closely. In fact, you will be blessed if both of you cling to the Lord, especially in the hard times (Psalm 63:8). Psalm 105 is an unsigned history of God's goodness and His wonderful works. His blessings and deliverance were displayed amidst troubling storms described by "Then they cried unto the LORD in their trouble" (Psalm 107:6, 13, 19, 28).

- *Good assurance available.* Make sure you have good insurance protectioncoverage for the stormy trials. Periodically it is wise to review your insurance policies with your agent. Making sure that you have the best protection in force will be really good when the storm is raging.

In your life and marriage, there is another policy that should be in force. This is your *assurance* policy. King David wrote of this when he said, "When my heart is overwhelmed: lead me to the rock that is higher than I. For Thou hast been a shelter for me...I will abide in Thy tabernacle forever: I will trust in the covert (shelter) of Thy wings. For Thou, O God, hast heard my vows" (Psalm 63:2, 4-5). God doesn't have literal wings. This does, however, illustrate that as the little chicks are sheltered from the storm under the outspread wings of the mother hen, so you can find shelter from your trial by abiding closely to the Lord.

- ***Remember that He knows how you feel.*** Maybe some well-meaning person has said to you, "I know just how you feel." Perhaps you have felt like screaming, "YOU DON'T KNOW HOW I FEEL, AND DON'T TELL ME THAT YOU DO!" Take a deep breath and take comfort in the fact that the Lord really *does* understand how you feel.

Think long about this: "For we have not an High Priest which cannot be touched with the feeling of our infirmities; but was in all points tempted like as we are, yet without sin. For such an High Priest became us, Who is holy, harmless, undefiled, separate from sinners, and made higher than the heavens" (Hebrews 4:15; 7:26).

So when you hear the careless words of a friend who glibly says, "Oh, I know just how you feel," (when in reality they have no idea what you are experiencing), just remember that the Lord Jesus, the great High Priest, understands you completely. The stormy trials will come into your life, marriage, or family. When they do, there is tremendous comfort in remembering that the Lord knows how you feel.

Think about these questions

1. Has anyone said to you, "I know how you feel"? How did it make you feel when your friend said that to you?

2. Have you and your spouse ever really stopped to think about the wonderful fact that our great Lord really does know just exactly how you feel?

The writer of the book of Hebrews declares that the Lord Jesus Christ has experienced everything that you will ever experience. The only thing He didn't experience was sinning. Every other situation was experienced by our Lord in His humanity. He understands you completely. What a blessing is yours to remember that the Lord Jesus Christ fully understands what you are going through; therefore, He can comfort you and sustain you in this storm.

- ***Bend the knee and bow the heart.*** Give your situation to the Lord. Be deliberate about surrendering it to Him. Bending the knee and bowing the heart is the intentional giving of self and situation to the Lord. It is the commitment to learn what He wants to teach you through the storm. It involves being willing to act on His leading. It will require obedience, faith, and purpose of heart. What a grand time for you and your spouse to talk about the situation and pray together about it!

The writer of the Book of Hebrews confidently states, "Let us therefore come boldly unto the throne of grace, that we may obtain mercy, and find grace to help in times of need" (4:15). King David provides rich counsel on how to give the hard times over to the Lord. He had a lot of experience with this. He said, "Cast thy burden upon the LORD, and He shall sustain thee: he shall never suffer the righteous to be moved" (Psalm 55:22). The Apostle Peter said, "Casting all your care upon Him; for He careth for you" (1 Peter 5:7).

Giving your situation to the Lord does not mean that you become idle and sit by, watching and waiting for the Lord to do everything. Giving the situation to the Lord is a deliberate decision to commit yourself to seeking His will and watching for His working. Picture yourself walking along trying to carry a load that is way too heavy. Picture yourself calling out to the Lord and asking Him to carry the load as He walks with you. He has the strength to carry it and the wisdom to resolve it!

What a powerful blessing will come to you and your spouse as you give your trial over to the Lord and ask Him to bear the heavy load!

Ask Him to give you comfort, wisdom, and strength as you are going through the stormy time.

- ***Choose joy.*** Do not allow this trial to rob you of joy. Do not allow this trial to push you and your spouse apart. Do not allow this trial to cause resentment toward the Lord to grow in your heart.

  The Apostle Peter understood hardships and trials. He encourages you by saying, "Beloved, think it not strange concerning the fiery trial which is to try you, as though some strange thing happened unto you: But rejoice, inasmuch as you are partakers of Christ's sufferings; that, when His glory shall be revealed, you may be glad also with exceeding joy" (1 Peter 4:12-13). There is joy that is available!

  Think of the difference between happiness and joy. Happiness depends on circumstances going the way you desire. Joy is very different from this. Joy does not depend on circumstances going the way that you would choose. Joy is a fruit of the Holy Spirit (Galatians 5:22-23), which is a special gladness that He desires to grow in your life in spite of trials. It comes through a personal relationship with the Giver of joy Whose name is the Lord Jesus Christ.

Tim and Marie discovered this joy in the midst of the trial through which they were traveling. Both knew the Lord Jesus as personal Savior. Just before Tim was wheeled into emergency surgery, Marie held his hand in the emergency room. Quietly Tim said to his young wife, "Sweetheart, we belong to the Lord Jesus. Let's remember that He is right here with us. Let's not miss any of the blessings that He has planned." Over the next several weeks of recovery, Tim and Marie, though hurting for each other, possessed a deep joy and encouraging gladness. Even though the trial was severe and the long recovery was fraught with difficulties, they both chose to let joy reign supreme in the midst of difficulty.

One evening Marie said to her husband, "Timmy, I am so glad that the Lord has given us more time together. I would never have chosen your emergency surgery, but deep in my heart there is such a joy and gladness that only He can give us. I am so thankful for His joy. It was hard to see you hurting physically, but I am glad for the joy He has given to us."

These principles are not a short list of quick fixes for when the storms of life strike. They are Biblical principles that are true, and they can be yours even in the greatest storms of life. As a believer, you can discover how these powerful principles help in times of trouble. If you will do them, you will experience help in the greatest storms. It takes more than simply knowing these principles. It is important to do them. The Lord Jesus said, "If ye know these things, happy are ye if ye do them" (John 13:17).

Wise homeowners have good insurance protection coverage on their home and great assurance plans for their marriage.

The Alarming Home Invasion

"Neither give place to the devil" (Ephesian 4:27).

Nothing strikes terror into the hearts of people any faster than to hear the term "home invasion." The broken glass, the forced door, the aggressive intruder, the violation of home privacy and security, the danger of injury or even death, and the get-away before the police can arrive leave emotional scars of fear, anger, and distrust for years. In the home invasion more than just property is stolen. The sense of safety, well-being, and security are the greatest losses.

The devil seldom operates in open boldness like the typical robber. He seldom is as obvious as breaking glass and forcing doors. He is sly and crafty. He usually operates in ways that careless people would never think of being the devil's fault. If he would just be honest and come right out and make it obvious that he wants to ruin your life and marriage, he could more easily be spotted and stopped. Satan often tries to get a foothold quietly and without a great deal of attention.

Have you ever heard of Omar and his camel? Omar slept in his tent, and, of course, his camel slept outside. Each evening the camel slept just a little closer to the tent. Omar paid little attention until the time came when his camel slept with his nose inside Omar's tent. "It's just his nose," said Omar and paid little attention. The next night the camel slept with his head inside the tent. "It's just his head," said Omar and paid little attention. The next night the camel slept with his head and neck in the tent.

Again Omar said, "It's just his head and neck," and paid little attention to it. Finally, the entire camel was in Omar's tent, sound asleep and thoroughly enjoying himself. Where's Omar? He's sleeping outside! Oh, how he wished that he had paid better attention, but it was too late! It would have been easier for our friend Omar to have dealt with his sneaky camel long before it was only his nose in the tent.

That's exactly how the devil works. He works in ways that people think "it's no big deal." Satan is sly and crafty. His purposes are destructive. He opposes that which is Godly and blessed.

Be on the alert for your enemy
The Apostle Paul warned the Ephesian believers "Neither give place to the devil" (Ephesians 4:27). Your enemy, the devil, very much wishes to break into your marriage. Often he will not smash in and enter by drawing attention to himself. He quietly and slowly creeps in by pushing you and your spouse away from each other. There are several words in this verse that provide the key to protecting against the unwanted intruder whose name is the devil.

- *"Give."* The first word is "give." This is the word *didomi* which means "of one's own accord to offer, to give of self, to set out and adventure in." You and your spouse must be very intentional on seeking wisdom from the Lord and being devoted to the Lord.

- *"Place."* The second word is "place." This is the word *topos* which means "any space marked off, a license to act, an opportunity, or an occasion to act."

So what is the Lord telling you through the Apostle Paul? It simply is this. Be deliberate. Know your enemy. Be alert as to how he works. Understand his method of operation. Then do not live carelessly by giving him a license to operate in your home, family, or marriage.

Stop and think about Paul's statement. Do not live in a careless manner. Do not give opportunities for the devil to take advantage or to seize opportunities to harm or ruin your marriage. Just as you would never leave windows unlocked and door open overnight, do not let your guard down when it comes to your enemy who hates you and anything that is Godly and represented in your home and marriage.

He is the great robber and will seek to destroy whatever he can.

There are a couple of things that you must accept as true, if you and your spouse are going to have genuine spiritual security.

Know your spiritual enemy

- *The devil is real.* He is not a cute, funny, little imaginary creature. His very name, devil, is "diabolos" which means "the accuser, the slanderer." Paul warned believers to "put on the whole armor of God that we might stand against the wiles of the devil." This speaks of his character and method of operation.

- *He has fallen from Heaven.* Take a moment to read about this in Isaiah 14:12-20. It might surprise you to know that he is still allowed temporary access before the Lord (Job 1:6; 2:1). In the middle of the future seven-year tribulation period, he will be cast from Heaven, never to be allowed back before God's throne (Revelation 12:7-9).

- *He is an accuser.* The Apostle John specifically called him the "accuser of our brethren" (Revelation 12:10). This means that the devil actually does accuse believers. Neither you nor your spouse is perfect. You are just like every other couple. Both of you, individually, and you as a couple, have made mistakes and sinned. John tells us that the devil apparently loves to make accusations against God's people.

Before you fall into despair, there is something marvelous to remember. You and your spouse can have the joy of knowing that Christ is your Advocate (1 John 2:1). The advocate is the defense attorney who represents the accused. What wonderful blessing to know that when the devil accuses the believer (hopefully you and your souse are living in such a way that there will be little of which the devil can accuse you), the Lord Jesus Christ is your Advocate. It is He Who paid your entire sin debt that answers any and all accusations from the devil.

- *He is slanderous.* "Then Satan answered the LORD, and said, Doth Job fear God for nought? Put forth Thine hand now, and touch all that he hath, and he will curse Thee to Thy face" (Job 1:9, 11). He is great at causing doubt, distrust, and jealousy. Even when sins are confessed to the Lord and forgiveness is sought from those you have offended, don't be surprised if times of guilt, perhaps even great guilt, come to your mind. And isn't it amazing how easy it is to remember all the hurts you have experienced from your spouse? Even when your spouse has genuinely apologized, how easy it is to still remember the hurt and hold the grudge. That's all part of the home invader robbing you of the joy of forgiveness and restoration.

- ***He is a murderer and a liar.*** "He was a murderer from the beginning and abode not in the truth because there is no truth in him" (John 8:44). He lied to our first parents, Adam and Eve. He deceived them (Genesis 3:1, 4-5). Because of their disobedience to God, death came into the human family. He likewise instigates lies to married couples today.

Here are the top ten lies that he whispers to married couples:

- If God really loved you, you would not be having these problems.
- You would be much happier if you walked out of your marriage.
- Your children will not be affected if you get a divorce. They can visit on the weekends and will do just fine.
- This is a different day and age than when the Bible was written. Get with it and enjoy being free to do whatever makes you happy.
- You deserve to be happy. Go and find it for yourself.
- God doesn't care about you. If He did care so much, why has this situation happened to you?
- You are wasting your time trying to serve the Lord. It isn't worth it.
- The Bible isn't God's Word. It's just a book of stories and myths.
- You are a failure, and your marriage is a failure. Everything you do is a failure. Give up.
- Your problems are impossible to solve. Just give up.

See your enemy for what he is. He is a one who greatly desires to destroy and kill everything that is beautiful about your marriage.

- ***The devil is a deceiver.*** "For such are false apostles, deceitful workers, transforming themselves into the apostles of Christ. And no marvel;

for Satan himself is transformed into an angel of light (2 Corinthians 11:13-14).

If only the devil was honest with people! He is very good at twisting things and making situations look good, logical, inviting, wholesome and even spiritual. Beware! Every situation must be viewed through the grid of God's Word. What does God's Word say? What does God's Word teach? What would the Lord Jesus do? God will never violate His Word.

- *The devil is a tempter.* "Then was Jesus led up of the Spirit into the wilderness to be tempted of the devil. And when He had fasted forty days and forty nights, He was afterward an hungered. And when the tempter came to Him, he said…(Matthew 4:1-3).

It is stunning! In fact, it is outrageous! Christ began his public ministry with His Father's affirmation of being well pleased with Him (Matthew 3:16-17). Immediately He is directed into the wilderness by the Holy Spirit to be tempted of the devil in three ways, according to Matthew 4.

First, the devil tempted Him concerning the desire of His flesh and the desire for food (4:3). Second, the devil tempted Him with the pride of life, saying that the angels would protect him if He would jump off the pinnacle of the temple (4:5-6). The devil even quoted Scripture in this temptation! That ought to give you and your spouse cause to stop and think carefully about your enemy. He can even twist and misuse Scripture! Third, the devil tempted Him with the lust of the eyes as the devil took Him into a high mountain and showed Him all the kingdoms of the earth. In an outrageously arrogant moment, the devil offered the Lord Jesus all these kingdoms, if He would bow down and worship him (4:8-10).

The Lord Jesus could have easily defeated the devil by His own authority; however, He did something that was far better and absolutely fantastic for us. In all three temptations the Lord Jesus answered by quoting Scripture. In the first temptation (4:4), He quoted Deuteronomy 8:3. In the second temptation (4:7), He quoted Deuteronomy 6:16. In the last temptation (4:10), He quoted Deuteronomy 6:13.

Why is this important to us? The answer is because this is how you and your spouse must answer sinful temptations when they come to you. And they will come to you! Do not think that you are somehow immune from his temptations. Never think that you are strong enough to answer the devil's temptations by your own wisdom or strength. The only way to answer the devil's temptations is to respond with appropriate Scripture.

The writer of Psalm 119 understood the power of God's Word. He declared, "Wherewithal shall a young man cleanse his way? By taking heed thereto according to Thy Word. With my whole heart have I sought Thee: let me not wander from Thy Commandments. Thy word have I hid in mine heart, that I might not sin against Thee" (Psalm 119:9-11).

Let's come back to a portion of God's Word shared earlier. Paul the apostle implored the Ephesian believers when he wrote, "Finally, my brethren, be strong in the Lord, and in the power of His might. Put on the whole armor of God, that ye may be able to stand against the wiles of the devil. For we wrestle not against flesh and blood, but against principalities, against powers, against the rulers of the darkness of this world, against spiritual wickedness in high places. Wherefore take unto you the whole armor of God, that ye may be able to withstand in the evil day, and having done all, to stand. Stand therefore (6:10-14a).

The psalmist declared, "Thy word is a lamp unto my feet, and a light unto my path" (Psalm 119:105). Throughout the lifetime of your marriage you will be faced with many decisions. Opportunities will come to you that will require significant decisions. You and your spouse may need to create a little dust by working on your marriage so that you can stay best friends after the honeymoon's over. It will be very important for you both to love God's Word, put on the whole armor of God, and make it a real part of your lives.

Adrianne loved her grandmother very much. Many of her best memories took her back to the times when she would see her grandmother reading the Bible. When Grandma went home to be with the Lord, Adrianne was given Grandma's Bible. It was a treasure as her beloved grandmother wrote many little notes in the margins of the Scriptures.

One day Adrianne discovered this little note in the margin of Psalm 119:

> The Word of God captures my attention (119:161);
> The Word of God corrects my actions (119:133);
> The Word of God controls my attitude (119:162-165).

That evening as Adrianne and her husband talked about her discovery, they thanked the Lord for the rich blessing they enjoyed as believers. Throughout their marriage they had been committed to making God's Word the priority. They understood that they had a spiritual enemy who wanted to invade their marriage and rob them of the blessing God wanted to give to them. They asked the Lord to give them wisdom to spot their enemy's temptation, diligence to be on guard against his attacks, and joy in their relationship with the Lord Himself. What a great goal and prayer for you and your spouse!

Wise homeowners take appropriate actions to make sure that their property is safe and secure. Nothing is more frightening or alarming than a home invasion. Viewing the devil as a home invader and taking him seriously is very wise.

The Scriptures give the believer very clear direction concerning this dreadful and dangerous enemy. You and your spouse must watch against him (2 Corinthians 2:11), fight against him in the power of the Lord (Ephesians 6:10-18), resist him (James 4:7), view him as an adversary (1 Peter 5:8), and overcome him through the power of the Lord Jesus Christ (1 John 2:13).

Think about these questions

1. Read Matthew 4:1-11. What are two or three lessons you can see from the temptation that the Lord Jesus faced?

2. How did the Lord Jesus answer each of the adversary's temptations?

3. What are two or three verses that you and your spouse have relied upon to help you to be overcomers against the wiles of the devil?

4. Do you and your spouse memorize God's Word? What does Psalm 119:9-11 say about this?

Those Pesky Little Bugs Can Eat Me Out of House and Home!

Marcia and Tim had a family of six boys. Each one of them had a great appetite. One day Marcia jokingly told her friend, Marietta, "Those boys of mine are eating me out of house and home!" Marietta looked back at her friend, and with a note of concern in her voice, said, "I wish it were only boys eating me out of house and home. Of all things, we have a termite infestation. I'm glad we caught it when we did, or they would have succeeded in eating me out of house and home!"

Obviously, termites are a serious problem. According to experts, they can be found in every state except Alaska and can cause billions in damage every year. Often they go undetected until damage is already taking place. That's probably why they are called 'pests'!

Not only do these pests exist in the physical world, there are spiritual pests as well. These spiritual pests are unwanted, uninvited, and many times go undetected until great damage is done that results in physical, emotional, financial, and spiritual consequences. As you build a beautiful marriage of lasting friendship, be alert for signs of these unwanted spiritual pests.

The very dangerous pest called pride

Pride is a terrible pest that robs of God's blessing. It is possible that a proud spirit can be harbored secretly without being detected immediately. But just like termites, sooner or later the evidence of this pest's presence will make itself known. What is pride? Basically pride is the feeling of being more important than others, being better than others, being more deserving than others, and of thinking more highly of one's self than one should.

Apparently such attitudes existed in the early church at Rome. The Apostle Paul declared, "For I say, through the grace that is given unto me, to every man that is among you, not to think of himself more highly than he ought to think; but to think soberly, according as God hath dealt to every man the measure of faith" (Romans 12:3).

James struggled with this throughout much of his lifetime. As a result, it became very difficult for him to form lasting relationships. In his pride and arrogance he pushed people away. His pride should have been a source of embarrassment in his life. His arrogance grew until it poisoned his marriage, estranged his family, and hurt his business tremendously.

That's exactly what the writer of the book of Proverbs was talking about when he wrote, "The fear of the Lord is to hate evil, pride, and arrogancy; and the evil way, and the froward mouth, do I hate" (8:13).

Pride and arrogance are among the things that God actually hates. The writer of Proverbs observed, "When pride cometh, then cometh shame" (11:2). In fact, Proverbs 29:23 declares, "A man's pride shall bring him low."

Be alert for this silent destructive pest called pride. Seeing ourselves as the Lord sees us will result in a healthy dose of humility.

The very destructive pest called envy

Margaret lived with jealousy and envy throughout much of her adult life. She frequently struggled with why her friends seemed to have things that she and her husband couldn't afford. There were times when their marriage was not nearly as happy as it could have been because of Margaret's envious spirit. Her husband Hank was getting to the point where he almost dreaded being home and around her. It seemed like nothing that he could do pleased her, even though he tried.

Then the day came that Margaret substituted in the church nursery. There before her very eyes, little envious Timothy eyed Samantha who was holding a toy that he wanted. Samantha had it. Timmy didn't. Samantha didn't even know he wanted it. Timmy kicked the wall, threw himself on the floor, pounded his little fists on the carpet, burst into tears and screamed at the top of his lungs, "I want it! I want it! I want it!"

While two other ladies in the nursery took care of the crisis, Margaret was struck with the fact that in a very real sense that was exactly how God must view her actions. Though she never threw herself on the carpet and pounded her fists, she had acted very much like this in her envious heart. She became convicted that her envy and jealousy were nothing less than sinful. Quietly she spoke to her husband and confessed her sin of envy and asked for his forgiveness. Together they asked the Lord to give them a sense of contentment and appreciation for His blessings. Thankfully it was not too late for them to deal with this serious spiritual pest.

The book of Proverbs is filled with dynamic principles and significant warnings to guide you and your spouse throughout your marriage. Envy is a very powerful spiritual pest and is described in Proverbs 27:4, "Wrath is cruel, anger is outrageous, but who is able to stand before envy?"

Paul told his precious coworker, Titus, "For we ourselves also were sometimes foolish, disobedient, deceived, serving divers (many, various) lusts and pleasures, living in malice and envy, hateful and hating one another (Titus 3:3).

Envy will rob you of contentment and joy in the Lord's provision. Do you or your spouse wrestle with envy? If so, take a good lesson from Timmy and Samantha in the church nursery!

Be alert for the pest called envy. Ask the Lord to give you contentment in Who He is and what He is doing in your life. Think of how He has provided your needs and even many of your wants.

The very dangerous pest called bitterness

Of all the things the Apostle Paul told the Ephesian believers to put away from them, he put bitterness at the head of the list. "Let all bitterness, and wrath, and anger, and clamor, and evil speaking, be put away from you, with all malice" (Ephesians 4:31). The word "bitterness" is *pikria* which has to do with "a poison or bitter root that leads to a wicked fruit in life."

This deep-seated resentment often is a secret hatred directed toward situations and people. Sometimes it can be concealed for long periods of time, yet it eats away at the joy and wellbeing of healthy relationships. It is best likened to a poison that eats away and slowly but surely results in a very destructive situation.

The writer of the book of Hebrews warns, "Looking diligently lest any man fail of the grace of God; lest any root of bitterness springing up trouble you, and thereby many be defiled" (Hebrews 12:15).

Bitterness will rob you of joy. It will take from you the peace that God wants to give you. The very blessings that God wants to bring into your life will be greatly hindered because of bitterness. Be on the alert for this destructive pest.

Harley deeply resented his older sister, Janet, and her husband, Vance. Neither realized Harley's resentment until the day a minor offense took place at a family reunion, of all places. Harley erupted into a tirade of foul language, screaming, and hurling accusations. Vance was stunned, and Janet felt crushed.

When Harley finally settled down, he told them of his bitterness that had grown for nearly a decade. "You got your dad's car, Vance. I had to buy my own. How do you think that makes me feel? Here you are with a car, and it didn't cost you a dime. But me? I had to go to the credit union for a loan."

By now the family reunion was ruined. Everyone was shocked. Janet left the room in tears. Quietly Vance turned to Harley and cleared his throat before speaking.

"Well, Harley, I've got to hand it to you. You surely know how to put a damper on a family reunion. First of all, why would you ever let such bitterness build up in your life? Second, why would you ever care what my dad and I do? Third, although it really is none of your business, my dad did not give me his car. He wanted to, but I told him that the only way I would take it is if he let me make payments on it. You can ask him. We paid for the car over a three year period of time. Bitterness surely is a rotten thing, Harley. I'm really sorry for you."

One of the sure dangers of bitterness is that the poison it causes will destroy your joy in the Lord's blessings, as well as distort your outlook. What a silly thing to cause Harley's bitterness! How foolish he acted because the root of bitterness had so long been growing!

Be alert for the pest called bitterness. The only cure for bitterness is confession of sin and forgiveness for offenses.

The very dangerous pest called stubbornness
Following the great conquest of the land and the ministry of Joshua came the period of the judges. The following observation is made in Judges 2:19,

"And it came to pass, when the judge was dead, that they returned, and corrupted themselves more than their fathers, and following other gods to serve them, and to bow down unto them, they ceased not from their own doings, nor from their stubborn way."

That's the problem with stubbornness! The same pattern, even though it is sinful and doomed to failure, is repeated over and over and over again. Stubbornness is often an unreasonable, unyielding, obstinate, fixed opinion or stated purpose.

Asaph wrote about his desire that his generation would be Godly and diligent in providing a good example to their children. He said, "That they might set their hope in God, and not forget the works of God, but keep His commandments. And might not be as their fathers, a stubborn and rebellious generation; a generation that set not their heart aright, and whose spirit was not steadfast with God" (Psalm 78:7-8).

Jenny fled to her mom and dad's house after Dan told her, "I don't know if I can take your stubbornness any longer. I just can't take it, Jen. I've had it."

The one person who seemingly could talk with Jenny without her being resentful had always been her dad. After listening to her story, Jenny's dad asked her to take a walk with him. He talked with her about her stubbornness and her unwillingness to listen to those who loved her. She bristled more and more, even though her dad had concrete examples to prove the veracity of his concerns.

Then the breakthrough came. Approaching the barnyard, several of his horses along with his mule stood nearby. "Watch this, Jen," her dad told her. As he walked into the barnyard, Jen's dad spoke quietly to his horses. Both horses followed the familiar farmer as he walked for a few moments around the barnyard. He warmly stroked both of his beloved pets, and there seemed to be a silent love between them.

He then came to the mule. Speaking to Stoney, he called for the mule to come. The mule didn't even lift his head. Jen's dad walked over to the mule, "Stoney, Stoney! Hey you! I'm talking to you." The mule never lifted his head. "I want you to come with me. Now!" Jen's dad, as he began to laugh, gently pretended to pull the beast. The mule never lifted his head. "Let me try this," Jen's dad called to her. Moving around behind the old mule, Jen's dad said, "Stoney! You must get moving!" as he pretended to give the mule a push.

Before her very eyes, almost as if he had read the script, old Stoney bellowed with a horrific screech, lifted his head, pushed back his ears, and kicked with his left rear hoof. Jen's dad jumped out of the way just in time.

Walking back to his daughter, Jen's dad took her face in his old weathered hands. "Jen, I will always love you. I am sure that Dan is certainly not perfect, nor is he always an easy man with whom to live. But Jenny dear, you are a very stubborn woman. Dan and the pastor are right. You are resisting, just as Stoney resisted me. You are hurting yourself, your marriage, and your family. It just doesn't have to be like this. Your stubbornness is causing much harm."

Jen looked at Stoney and burst into tears of repentance. Falling into her father's arms, she sobbed into his shoulder. Finally, the Lord broke through her stubbornness, and He used a donkey to do it.

Be alert for the pest called stubbornness. The cure for stubbornness is a consistent quickness to obey and a willingness to do what the Lord wants you to do.

The very dangerous pest called ingratitude

Read through the book of Psalms and watch for the many times we are instructed to give thanks unto the Lord. Just a very few of these would include:

- "I will give thanks unto the Lord among the heathen, and sing praises unto thy name" (Psalm 18:49).
- "Sing unto the LORD, O ye saints of His, and give thanks at the remembrance of His holiness" (Psalm 30:4).
- "Know ye that the LORD is God: it is He that hath made us, and not we ourselves; we are His people, and the sheep of His pasture. Enter into His gates with thanksgiving, and into His courts with praise: be thankful unto Him, and bless His name (100:3-4).

This matter of Thanksgiving is certainly not limited to the Psalms. The phrase "give thanks" is found in 39 verses in the KJV translation of the Bible. Thanksgiving and the expression of appreciation is a characteristic of genuine Christianity.

Perhaps one of the most striking illustrations of ingratitude is given in Luke 17:11-19. You remember the situation, don't you? Ten lepers cried out to the Lord Jesus and pled for healing. Jesus directed them to go and show themselves to the priest, and they were cleansed as they went. Perhaps all of the ten were thankful; however, only one returned to give thanks. Only one!

Read the response of the Lord Jesus to this, "And Jesus answering said, Were there not ten cleansed? But where are the nine? There are not found that returned to give glory to God, save this stranger. And he said unto him, Arise, go thy way: thy faith hath made thee whole" (Luke 17:17-19). Imagine it! Ten lepers miraculously cleansed; only one returned to give thanks.

Paul the great apostle wrote to his beloved son in the faith, Timothy, and warned him that in the last days perilous times would come. These days would be marked by those who would be "lovers of their own selves, covetous, boasters, proud, blasphemers, disobedient to parents, unthankful, unholy" (2 Timothy 3:1-2). The sin of ingratitude and being unthankful is so hurtful and destructive. It is a very serious spiritual pest.

Would people close to you be able to say that you are a thankful person? Do you express appreciation to your spouse? Are you quick to say "thank you" when people bless your life? Does your great and awesome God hear you express your heartfelt thanksgiving to Him?

Beware of the pest called ingratitude. The way to rid yourself of this pest is a growing sense of appreciation to the Lord. A thankful spirit and a heart that praises the Lord will help you to overcome this terrible pest.

These and many other little pests can cause great damage in marriages.

Come to think of it, that's the problem with pests. They don't knock on the door. They are sometimes difficult to spot. They often go unnoticed while they create significant harm and destruction. You need to be diligent. Be on guard. Be watching for them, and be quick to respond.

There is good news about the pests

While no one wants any of these or other pests, the good news about pests is that once you are aware of them, they can be prevented or stopped. The following is not a list of quick fixes for spiritual pests; however, in these Biblical principles, God provides for us the wonderful opportunity to overcome and stop the pests in their tracks.

- Ask the Lord to help you spot any undetected sinful pest (Psalm 139:23-24).
- Acknowledge the presence of any sinful pest discovered by you (Psalm 51:3-4).
- Confess to the Lord your sin, and view it as a destructive, dangerous pest (1 John 1:9).
- Be honest with your spouse, acknowledging the harmful effects of your sinful pest and seek restoration by asking for forgiveness. Do not delay in doing this (Matthew 5:24).
- Actively and aggressively take the spiritual steps to correct the situation and defeat the spiritual pest (Romans 6:1-22). These steps include the following: First, arrest yourself by seeing the seriousness of your sin (verse 1). Second, revoke your license to sin, and do not allow yourself to continue in it (verse 2). Third, picture your participation with the Lord Jesus Christ in his death, burial and resurrection (verse 3). Fourth, reckon yourself to be dead unto this sin, and yield yourself completely to God (verses 11-13). Last, do not think that it is impossible to get rid of this sinful pest. God has great plans for you (Verses 14-22).
- Daily submit yourself to the Lord Jesus Christ (Matthew 11:28-30).
- Understand that with the help of the Lord Jesus, you really can have victory (Philippians 4:13).

Wise homeowners understand that there will certainly be the onslaught of storms. They also understand that there is the very real possibility of a home invasion; therefore, they take necessary precautions. Unless they live in the state of Alaska, homeowners in every state need to be on guard for the pest called termites.

The same will be true in marriages. There will be times that storms will come along. The devil is certainly a great adversarial marriage invader. Sinful actions are very similar to termites. Sometimes they are hard to detect, but always they result in great destruction.

Your marriage is very much like a house. Do not allow the storms to push you and your spouse apart. Rather, let them draw you and your spouse closer to each other and closer to the Lord. Do not give place to your enemy, the devil. View him as a powerful, deceptive, lying enemy who wants to invade your marriage and harm it. Be on guard for spiritual pests that result in sinful actions and attitudes. They will harm your marriage.

Think about these questions

Talk them over with your spouse. How would you answer the following?

1. What would be the greatest stormy trial through which you have traveled with your spouse?

2. What are some of the lessons God taught you from this stormy trial?

3. In what ways are you safeguarding yourself and your marriage from giving any place to the devil?

4. Are you aware of any spiritual pest in your personal life? How would your spouse answer this about you?

Our Prayer for Our House and Marriage

Lord, we want our house to stand against the greatest gale.
We enjoy the safe refuge from the rain and wind beating
relentlessly upon it.
We want to secure and protect both our house and marriage
from any potential enemy intruder.
We want to learn to be wise in fortifying our house and marriage
from anyone or anything that would be harmful.
We remember that little pests create great destruction.

So we thank you, Lord, for each other and for our marriage.
Our marriage is of far greater significance than any house can ever be.
When hard times come, please help us to draw closer to each other.
May the hard times not push us apart.
Lord, You are our God in the good times, and You are to be
trusted in the hard times.
May the storms draw us closer to You, Lord.
The devil truly is our absolutely terrible enemy.
He is a thief, a robber, a murderer, and a liar.
May he never be welcomed in our home or marriage, Lord.
As for those little pests that can create great damage,
help us to realize that we are totally capable
of having any or all of those pests operate in our lives.
These pests are sinful.
Lord, please help us to be serious
and remember that sin always is destructive and harmful.

May we ever take it seriously! Amen!

It is my prayer that there will be a little "dust" which is the evidence that you are working in this area in your marriage. Constructing a beautiful marriage is a lot like constructing a beautiful house!

Chapter Seven
Overcoming Procrastination

Fix the Little Things Before They Become Big

"A little leaven leavens the whole lump" (Galatians 5:9)

*"It's just a little thing.
It surely won't matter that much," he thought.
But the little thing became a slightly bigger thing.
Still unaddressed, the slightly bigger thing became a much bigger thing.
It would have been so easy to fix it when it was a smaller thing.
"I sure wish I had paid attention to the smaller thing
before it became a big thing," he said.*

From Grandpa's note: Repair broken things right away. Better to fix something when it is little than put it off until it is big and costly.

Key thought: *The problem with procrastination is that the day of reckoning eventually catches up with you, and often things are worse for waiting. This putting off the fixing of little things will eventually become the fixing of big things.*

Ken and Alisha ran into Hank Mitchell and his wife at the grocery store about a year after the completion of the building of their new house. "Hey! How nice to see you once again, Mr. Mitchell," Ken said as he reached his hand out to shake Hank's.

"Well, well, well, and how are Ken and Alisha and that new house of yours?" Hank replied, nearly dropping his bag of groceries. After introducing the young couple to his wife, with a jesting tone in his voice he said, "I hope nothing has already broken down in that new house of yours."

"No, sir," Alisha was quick to reply. "But you have to remember that we had--what's their names? Oh yes, I remember, we had the Mitchell and Sons Construction team. We hear that their houses last a lifetime with no repairs!" she said teasingly.

"Well, ma'am," Hank choked, "I would say you must've been pretty impressed with some kind of sales pitch somewhere or another! Seriously, I am convinced that our houses are constructed well. But do you know what? I found that most repairs when caught right away are much easier to fix than those that are ignored for a while. When it comes to fixing things, it's easier to deal with the little than with the big. My kids are always teasing me and saying to me that I can turn every situation into a little sermon. Sorry about that! But our houses are a lot like marriages. Procrastination will hurt both house and marriage," Hank said with sincerity.

"Thanks, Mr. Mitchell. We will most certainly do that, and it was great to see you again," Ken assured Henry Mitchell.

Such Sad Situations

Perhaps you have made some of the following same excuses for procrastinating. Consider these procrastinators. Their situations didn't go away. They caught up later and were bigger than ever.

"I probably ought to do something about this, but it's such a little thing that maybe if I ignore it, it will go away. If it doesn't go away, I will fix it when I get around to it." This is the sad thinking of people in dozens of situations.

"I'll get to the doctor sometime," he said. "Right now I'm busy," and so the man ignored a growing medical situation.

"We ought to do something sometime," said the students who ignored a growing tension toward a student who was being bullied.

Overcoming Procrastination

"Our marriage isn't working. We've both changed. We need to get help and get this straightened out sometime," said the couple whose marriage went from aggravation to fracture.

The medical situation became critical. The school student tried to kill himself. The couple ended in divorce court. All three shared a commonality. Their problems started small, but they were ignored. As the troubles grew, all three continued to ignore and repress them. Finally, when the situation was ready to explode, help was sought.

These situations became much more difficult to deal with because of one word—procrastination. Each person put off dealing with the issues until it was nearly too late. That's why procrastination is so serious.

Understand the Definition

So how would you define procrastination? What is the difference between sinful procrastination and spiritual waiting on the Lord?

Waiting on the Lord is active anticipation

Waiting on the Lord is very different from procrastination. The Psalmist declares, "Wait on the LORD: and he shall strengthen thine heart: wait, I say, on the LORD" (27:14). David uses the word *qavah*, which gives the idea of "waiting on God with eagerness for His answer." This waiting is in anticipation of what only God can do. You don't know how God will answer your prayer, so you wait and watch. With faith and trust in Him, you read His Word. You invest extra time seeking His will. You watch for God to work and to give you wisdom to know what you should do. Waiting is an active anticipation.

Procrastination is deliberate delaying

Procrastination is the deliberate delay of or putting off a response to a particular situation. This is especially serious when the situation demands and requires immediate attention. Procrastination is not accidental. It is not spiritual to pretend to be waiting upon the Lord. Procrastination is a deliberate action. Specifically, it is a choice to ignore the situation, diminish its seriousness, or pretend the situation does not exist.

Wise homeowners understand that leaky roofs are not going to suddenly fix themselves. Dripping faucets are not going to go away. Peeling paint will fall to the ground and not fix itself! Procrastinating homeowners routinely go from small repairs that require a lot less effort and expense in repair to the final "now we have a big problem" kind of necessary repair.

Paul's Great Illustrations

The Apostle Paul was an excellent speaker and communicator of God's truth. One of the things he frequently employed in his writing was the use of great illustrations. In the text of Galatians chapter five, he uses two pictures or illustrations that will help you understand the seriousness of procrastination.

The picture of a runner

The believers in the churches in the region of Galatia began well in their Christian life. They were like the athlete who runs the race in grace, carrying nothing else that would weigh him down (5:7). Tragically, another runner stepped into their lane, demanding they return to legalism. This legalism was a false doctrine that could sidetrack the church at Galatia, so Paul reminded them to be running the race in grace alone.

Paul's first illustration of procrastination dealt with this legalism. It was the unnecessary and even sinful baggage being strapped on the back of a runner. That would be unthinkable.

The writer of the book of Hebrews wrote of the serious consequences of runners being weighed down. "Let us lay aside every weight, and the sin which doth so easily beset us, and let us run with patience the race that is set before us, Looking unto Jesus the author and finisher of our faith" (Hebrews 12:1b-2a). Think of the runner and imagine what problems procrastination would cause. Paul warned not to let anything infringe upon the successful race set before them as runners. Laying aside unnecessary weight demanded immediate attention. Procrastination leads to potential disaster for those in a race. Listen to the voice of procrastination in runners:

- I don't want to go to the gym today. I'll go tomorrow, maybe.
- I don't want to diet today. I'll start eating better tomorrow, maybe.

- I don't want to run today. I'll run tomorrow, maybe.
- It's not nice outside today. It'll be nicer tomorrow, maybe.
- I'm tired of training today. I'll train twice as hard tomorrow, maybe.

Perhaps procrastinating for a day or even two would not result in disaster. That's not the point. The real point is that it is easier for a runner to put off the difficult, even if it risks disaster and defeat, until tomorrow, rather than face it today and overcome it!

The picture of the baker

Bakers use leaven and will immediately recognize Paul's second illustration. Often the Scriptures depict leaven as a picture of wickedness or sin. During the Passover no leaven was allowed in the entire house (Exodus 12:15-19; 13:7). The worshippers of the Lord were not typically permitted to mingle leaven with their sacrifices (Exodus 34:25). Our precious Lord used leaven as an illustration of sin when He warned His listeners about the leaven of the Pharisees (Matthew 15:6-12).

Leaven is a little thing, yet if left unattended, it slowly but surely grows and permeates the entire lump of dough. That is exactly what sin does. Often it is viewed as a little matter, of no great significance, but when sin is unconfessed and left to itself like leaven, it will grow, and the results will be much harder with which to deal. This is so true in the area of home, marriage, and the family.

The practical application for you and your spouse

What does running and baking have to do with successful marriages resulting in best friendships? The answer is that they have more to do with this than many folks would think or like to acknowledge! If you are a runner, you know that you don't dare procrastinate when it comes to diligence and training. A day or two off here or there, a fattening dessert here and there, and a training day skipped here and there, and soon there is an out-of-shape runner who is not able to compete at Olympic levels.

Likewise, if you view any sin as little, innocent, insignificant, or "it's not as bad as someone else's sin," there's big trouble brewing. It's just a little leaven or yeast that is used, and yet somehow it affects the whole lump of dough. Its presence, though unseen at first, will be evident before long.

Wise believers understand that there's no such thing as a little sin. We tend to categorize sins, and if we haven't murdered, stolen thousands from our employer, or committed adultery with our neighbor's spouse, then we aren't doing badly. Satan has always been the master deceiver. The Lord Jesus cautions regarding the devil when He says, "He was a murderer from the beginning, and abode not in the truth, because there is no truth in him. When he speaketh a lie, he speaketh of his own: for he is a liar, and the father of it" (John 8:44).

Satan is such a liar. He perpetrates on individuals and marriages two great lies. Lie number one is, "It's only a little sin; it's no big deal, and everyone does it." Lie number two is, "There's plenty of time to fix it; relax, it's no big deal; you have plenty of time; work on it another day."

You are in a race! Don't procrastinate in areas of self-discipline. As you live for the Lord, picture sin as the leaven or yeast that affects the entire lump of dough. The application of this truth to the runner and the baker illustrates that sin must be taken seriously, and it must be taken seriously immediately.

Fix It Early or Pay More Later

Even the most beautiful of houses requires upkeep and will encounter necessary repairs. Likewise, even great marriages have situations that arise. Often these situations begin as small little nuisances. It is possible that the offending spouse may not even be aware of the situation. When the wounded spouse speaks to the offending spouse about the situation, sometimes the response is something like, "You've got to be kidding me. I don't remember saying that. I don't remember ever doing that. Do you really mean that silly little thing actually hurt your feelings?" It is possible that your spouse may view the situation as minor and that someday he or she will work on it.

When it happens again, the wounded or offended spouse thinks something like, "My spouse is never going to change." Now the minor nuisance grows into an aggravation which results in a deepening offense. It is no longer just a nuisance. Resentment builds, and if left unchecked, grows into anger.

Your situation is not new, nor is it unique to you. From four decades of marital counseling, I have discovered that big marital problems often started out as little things that were left unchecked, undealt with, and unresolved. Once a little thing, then easily repaired, now had grown into a much larger thing and was much more difficult to fix.

Do any of these statements sound like situations in your marriage?

- When we first started out, we had the attitude that it's all about "we and us." But now with my spouse it's "all about me and what I want." Where did our sense of sharing and caring go?

- When we first started out, we had wonderful passion and sex. Now we have sex, but absolutely no passion. Where did our intimacy go?

- When we first started out, we had great communication. Now we talk, but it is about meaningless things. Where did our times of communication go?

- When we first started out, we enjoyed spending time together. Now we have clocks in every room, but no time for each other. Where has our connection gone?

- When we first started out, we had very little income, very little savings, and very little material things, but we were so happy. Now we work longer hours, have so much stuff that it hardly fits into our house, and yet we are more deeply in debt than ever. Where did our contentment go?

- When we first started out, we greatly desired to have children. Now we have children, and we dearly love them, but they are taking our entire focus. We have no energy left for each other. Where did our alone time go?

- When we first started out, we had a lot of problems as we discovered just who we really married, but we talked about them. Then we came to the point that we put off dealing with them because we were so busy. Now we just ignore them. What a wall we have built up. Where did our honesty go?

Are any of these situations comparable to what's happening in your marriage? Let's ask the hard question. Are you aware of any situation that needs to be resolved, but you or your spouse are procrastinating and putting off working on it?

While every marriage is unique, you share commonalities with other couples. There seem to be several typical small situations that, if left unattended, result in bigger, more difficult-to-resolve problems. Do you see yourself and your marriage in any of these couples?

Meet Three Procrastinating Couples and Their Regrets

Pastor Kenward would be seeing three couples this week. These three couples would present situations that commonly occur in marriages that could have been fixed much more easily if addressed much earlier. All three couples professed knowing Christ as their personal Savior. These three couples were members in good standing in the church he serves. On the outside, things looked fine, but a brewing and festering situation was taking place in each marriage which was being ignored and put off. It's the old procrastination problem in full bloom in each of the marriages.

Meet Stan and Maggie who procrastinated with wrong priorities

Soon after Pastor Kenward came to their church, Stan made the remark, "Sometime my wife and I ought to come in and see you." Pastor Kenward had assured him that he would be happy to see them anytime. Now four years later Stan and Maggie are sitting in the pastor's office.

"We've got troubles, Pastor," Stan began. "We started out with the attitude of it being all about us--all about each other. We were in this marriage together. I wanted to be the kind of husband that would bless her. She wanted to be the same for me as my wife. Slowly that started changing. Now it has become more of a 'me, myself, and I' situation with both of us. We've lost the sense of our marriage being important. We aren't special to each other any longer. I don't want to hurt her, but Maggie has plenty of time and money for her friends and activities. What little time and money is left over seems to be going toward the kids. We love our children, but they have taken over and are making demands of us," Stan continued. "We are in big trouble," Stan said as he suddenly sobbed.

"I told Stan we should come to see you two years ago," Maggie said with a note of irritation in her voice. She looked over at her husband and then back to the pastor as she continued talking, "All I ever heard is 'We'll get 'round to it, Mag,' until I finally told him that if he didn't come, that's fine. I don't want to sit around the house all week as he works more and more. I am not spending money, and my friends are here at church. I go to a Bible study once a week and then down to the mission once every other week. Stan has gotten to the point where he is even more demanding than the children. We don't have time for each other, and when we do, we are at each other's throat. He no longer trusts me and says I'm spending our money on my friends. How silly. What has happened to us?"

Stan tried to explain, but Maggie interrupted him. "Stan, let me finish. Pastor, when we were first married, Stan was the most thoughtful man you could ever meet." She started crying as she continued, "He was still thoughtful when Kathryn came. Then the twins, Matthew and Silas, were born a little over a year later. I was changing diapers faster than I could keep up with some days. Now the twins are seven, and Kathy will be nine in several months. We are running more and more to try and keep the boys in sports because that is what Stan wants. Why would any seven-year-old have to play football? They don't even enjoy football, but Stan insists.

"Furthermore Pastor, Stan accuses me of spending money on myself and my friends. How dare he make such an accusation? If you want to know about spending money, ask him how much his golf costs! Ask him about the tickets to Sunday's game. He's not even going to be in church because he wants to go to the game. I am just sick of how his priorities have changed!" Maggie said as she choked through her tears.

As Maggie was about to say something else, Stan spoke out. "Yeah, that's true that I do want them in sports. But what about you? Why is Kathy taking piano lessons, saxophone lessons, and singing in two different choirs? Pastor, it isn't that Kathy wants to do all this. Her mother wants her be some kind of super musician."

Pastor Kenward hushed both of them.

Early in their marriage, their focus and priority had been each other. Slowly the priority and focus had begun to shift from each other to their children and then onto what they wanted for their children. As time went on, the feeling of emptiness grew as both Stan and Maggie no longer felt important to each other. Sadly, rather than talking with each other about this when the problem was small and easily correctable, they procrastinated, and now the problem was nearly insurmountable.

Don't procrastinate dealing with wrong priorities

You don't want to be in their situation, do you? To avoid being like Stan and Maggie, there are several things to seriously consider about procrastination.

- *Commit to the Lord's commands.* The Lord Jesus powerfully taught about the seriousness of wrong priorities in Matthew 5:23-24. He said, "Therefore if you bring your gift to the altar, and there remember that your brother has something against you, leave your gift there before the altar, and go your way. First be reconciled to your brother, and then come and offer your gift." (NKJV)

Wait a minute! Nothing should be more important than bringing my gift of worship to the Lord. Doesn't that sound right? Unfortunately, that is a wrong statement! It would seem that the Lord Jesus made it pretty clear that while worship is precious, others and your treatment of them must be an important priority, too. Did you notice the urgency and seriousness that He put into the situation? "First be reconciled" speaks of doing this immediately. Don't put it off. Don't procrastinate with priorities.

The Lord Himself and then others around you must have a high priority in your heart and life. The Lord Jesus said, "Thou shalt love the Lord thy God with all thy heart, and with all thy soul, and with all thy strength, and with all thy mind; and thy neighbor as thyself" (Luke 10:27). While God must have the first or highest priority, the love we have for others is a great priority as well.

Think of how this priority that you must have for your spouse and your marriage will play out in your life. The Apostle Paul declared,

"Submitting yourselves one to another in the fear of God." He then explained how this is demonstrated by the wife in her submission and respect to her husband as illustrated by the church (Ephesians 5: 22-24). He then explained how this is demonstrated by the husband in his sacrificial love and devotion to his wife as illustrated by the Lord Jesus Himself (Ephesians 5:25-27).

Think about these questions

1. What does Matthew 22:36-38 say about your relationship with the Lord?

2. What does Ephesians 5: 21-33 say about your relationship with your spouse? (Did you especially notice verse 21?)

3. What does Genesis 33:5, Deuteronomy 6:1-7, and Proverbs 3:11-12 say about your relationship with your children?

   - ***Commit to seeking God's will.*** David demonstrated such profound wisdom when he wrote, "I delight to do Thy will, O my God" (Psalm 40:8). God offers such powerful help for you if you are struggling with setting the right priorities. Significant distractions are all around you. These miserable little gremlins rob you of right priorities. They mask themselves as harmless little things that don't need immediate attention, but they are not harmless. They are selfishness, jealousy, anger, revenge, self-centeredness, pride, arrogance, and hardness of heart.

   While these gremlins are not instantly removed by a simple little one-time prayer, it is amazing to see what the Lord does in the life of a believer who prays and asks the Lord to make His will discernible and delightful.

   Imagine the amazing power that comes when you and your spouse kneel together before the Lord and seek His will for your marriage, home, family, work, and ministry opportunities that come to you. How important it is to have right priorities.

Paul strongly reminded the believers in the church at Rome, "And be not conformed to this world: but be ye transformed by the renewing of your mind, that ye may prove what is that good, and acceptable, and perfect will of God" (Romans 12:2). You cannot improve upon the will of God.

- **Commit to the Lord's wisdom.** Two of the most important things in life would be your marriage partner and your children. Your spouse and your children require special wisdom.

When their children came, Stan and Maggie started to have trouble dealing with right priorities. Can you relate to this?

Several couples were talking about raising their children. One parent said to another, "Yeah, having kids is tough. The problem is that these kids come, but they don't have directions on how to raise them." Sadly that statement brought a chuckle and much agreement; however, nothing could be further from the truth. Children do come with instructions.

God's wisdom, as revealed in God's Word, provides abundant guidance and direction in child-rearing. The Lord knows how to raise your children. Ask Him. Listen to this very good advice. "If any of you lack wisdom, let him ask of God" (James1:5).

Can you think of specific times that you asked the Lord for wisdom and later you were amazed at how the Lord worked out the situation? Are you still asking the Lord for His wisdom?

- **Commit to allowing your children to enjoy their childhood.** It is fine for children to play in sports or take up music, if this is the desire and inclination of your child. The writer of Proverbs spoke of a very important aspect that some parents overlook. He said, "Train up a child in the way he should go" (Proverbs 22:6). Every child must be trained in the way of the Lord; however, every child must be allowed to excel in the areas in which God has equipped.

How sad to watch a child struggling as he or she endeavors to win the approval and affection of an unwise parent. This parent expects and nearly demands the child to love things that are special to the parent but not to the child. Can you see the young boy whose dad wants him in every sport? The young boy hates sports. He wants to play the piano. "Wrong priorities!" screams out at the dad who insists on his own way.

Children will grow up quickly. While it is important for your children to learn how to know the Lord, how to follow God's way, how to respect other people, how to manage finances, how to do well in school, and a dozen other things, don't forget that children need to be children! They need to enjoy their childhood. They need to play and mature. They need to discover the inclinations the Lord has built into them.

- ***Commit to making your spouse your priority.*** Next to the Lord, your spouse ought to be the most important person in your life. Seek to find new, creative, and meaningful ways to demonstrate that your spouse is cherished. Don't be boring. Don't assume that your spouse knows of your love. Show your spouse. Let your spouse know by intentional, deliberate actions of his or her priority in your life.

Still speaking to the believers in the church of Rome, Paul also reminds us that the Lord didn't assume that we knew He loves us. In Romans 5:8 Paul wrote, "But God commended His love toward us, in that, while we were yet sinners, Christ died for us." The key principle you must grasp in this verse is that genuine love has a high priority. It must be demonstrated. It must be practiced.

Think about these questions

1. How did the Lord Jesus demonstrate His love for you?

2. How do you demonstrate your love for your spouse?

Remember back before your children arrived? What was your relationship like? Even though children are a great blessing, they do add a lot to any household schedule! Your marriage can have the highest priority even after your children come. It will require determination, cooperation, and coordination with your mate.

You must continue dating. You must continue investing. Don't stop laughing. Watch for the humor, and by all means, continue snuggling. Of course, because of your love for the Lord, continue worshipping and praying together. Wise couples who stay best friends long after the honeymoon's over will continue sharing secrets and making plans. Little things become memory-builders. Special days stay special. Anniversaries, birthdays, special days are never forgotten or missed. Continue parenting together, but don't let it rob you of making your marriage a priority.

- **Commit to speaking Biblically.** Wise couples with right priorities speak honestly but lovingly. Schedules often fill up, activities continue to mount up, busyness continues to pile up, and then it can happen. Either or both spouses can come to the point of explosion. Tensions soar, and words fly out. Sometimes it is not so much what is said but how it is said that causes the deep wound.

  As you and your spouse pray about the priorities of your home and family, be sure to be "Speaking the truth in love" (Ephesians 4:15). Spouses who are deeply in love with the Lord and each other know that the matter of right priorities needs constant attention.

Meet Leslie and Courtney who procrastinated with sinful choices

Les and Court, as their friends called them, moved across the country so that Les could take a promotion in the corporation in which he worked. Pastor Kenward had been their pastor for a little less than a year when they made their appointment to come and see him. Though the pastor and congregation had been very kind, genuinely gracious, and deeply cared about them, Leslie and Courtney were cool toward him and the rest of the congregation. They were sharp with each, and often seemed aloof. No one really seemed to get to know them as typically they were the first to leave after the services.

After Pastor Kenward invited them into his office and warmly welcomed them, he motioned for them to have a seat in the two chairs in front of his desk, but Courtney pulled her chair away from being close to Leslie's. They both sat in silence after Pastor finished his prayer. Neither talked, nor did they look up from staring at the floor. The silence grew awkward.

Finally Pastor Kenward said, "Well, folks, you asked to meet with me. How may I help you? What's on your minds? Les, you are the spiritual leader of your home, why don't you start."

"That's the whole problem," Courtney blurted out. "That's the whole problem. You hit the nail on the head, Pastor Kenward. Bingo! I can't believe we are here less than one minute, and already you have nailed it. Les is supposed to love me as Christ loved the church and gave Himself for it. But believe you me, Pastor, that isn't happening. He's no spiritual leader. We have drifted so far from the Lord and each other that it is pathetic, Pastor Kenward," Courtney fumed angrily with tears welling up in her eyes.

"That's Court for you, Pastor," Les said with a tone of resentment. Looking at her with anger written all over his face, he continued speaking, "She surely speaks her mind. That's the problem. She talks at me but never with me. She is never satisfied with anything. We weren't always like this, Pastor, but for the last five years of our marriage, we have been sinking." Looking back at the pastor and then looking down in defeat, Les told the pastor, "As miserable as she has become, I do blame myself.

"As I took on more responsibility at work, I came under more and more pressure. I wanted to come home and relax. I didn't want to talk. I didn't want to hear about problems. I didn't want to hear of her comparing me to her father. I allowed her to push me away to the point where, I'm ashamed to admit it, but I have been sinning, Pastor, badly sinning. We talk, but we don't communicate. We have sex rarely anymore, and even then, we don't have intimacy," Leslie quietly said.

Les kept looking down while slowly shaking his head. "At first I tried to please her. It became obvious that I would never live up to the comparison of her father. He is a wonderful man, Pastor, but nothing I ever did would ever match her father. Her tirades pushed me away. I should have gone to our pastor back east. Maybe I could have saved myself and our marriage a lot of heartache, if only I had gotten help early on. But as I said, I moved away emotionally," Les confessed.

"Go on, tell him. I want to hear you tell him, you miserable failure," Courtney demanded.

It had been a long time since the pastor had witnessed such a sudden onslaught of venom. After getting Courtney under control, the pastor's heart felt broken as he turned to Les and said, "Tell me what, Leslie."

Leslie sat before his pastor and suddenly crumpled in sorrow and shame. The tears came like a flood.

"It's my fault, Pastor. I take the full responsibility. Court wanted to get help as I began getting busier at work, and she started feeling lonelier. Her dad is a well-known judge who carries an enormous caseload, yet he obviously loves my mother-in-law and is an exceptional dad to his seven children. But I have failed miserably. I let Court's hurtful comparison drive me away. At first I turned to on-line pornography. Then it became the playful flirting with Allyson at work. Allie made me laugh. I thought she made me happy. Before I knew it we were in an immoral relationship. A week ago Court found out," Leslie said sobbing.

Before Courtney could speak or Leslie could say anything else, a shaken Pastor Kenward softly spoke and took control of the meeting. He began by determining that the immoral affair indeed was over. Les assured him that it was and shared with the pastor that he had phoned Allyson in Courtney's presence to tell her that it was over.

Pastor Kenward lovingly invested the rest of that evening, three more evenings that week, the full Saturday morning and then the next six months to help rebuild the devastated marriage of Les and Court.

It surely would have been a lot easier if both Les and Courtney had stopped making poor choices before they became sinful ones.

Don't procrastinate with disappointments, poor choices, and sinful actions. The Apostle Paul made an interesting statement under the inspiration of the Holy Spirit. He said, "Neither give place to the devil. Let him that stole steal no more: but rather let him labor, working with his hands the thing which is good, that he may have to give to him that needeth" (Ephesians 4:27-28).

Giving place to the devil brings the idea of making it easy for him to operate. When Leslie and Courtney were in the early years of their marriage, neither pleased the Lord. Courtney nagged and criticized her husband as she compared him to her father. Les never was a spiritual leader in his marriage even though they went to premarital counseling and learned of the importance of their roles. As both lived in ways that easily gave place to the devil, the wall between them continued growing. They talked but seldom really communicated. They rarely had sexual relations, and even then it was much more of a physical act than the joy of intimacy and passion.

The illustration of the thief stopping his stealing spree, getting a job, and then sharing generously with others who have needs is an incredible, opposite change of intention and direction. Robbers want to get quick gains for personal pleasure without working. Income to be shared with others as a result of hard work is as opposite to burglary as it can be. This is the radical change of heart that the Lord greatly desires to bring into your marriage.

Is there a disappointment that exists in your marriage that is festering and leading to the erection of a wall between you and your spouse? Are either you or your spouse on a course that is marked by sinful choices? Often these choices escalate into bigger issues and deeper sinfulness.

Don't procrastinate putting off sinful choices

Consider several things carefully. While this is not a list of quick fixes, these truths will help you to correct poor choices before they become bigger sinful choices.

- *The Lord is coming.* The Lord's soon return should stir you as a wise believer to pure living. "We know that, when he shall appear, we shall be like Him; for we shall see Him as He is. And every man that hath this hope in him purifieth himself, even as he is pure" (1 John 3:2-3).

  It is a great exercise of the heart to stop and think about the Rapture of the Church. It could occur at any moment. Picture yourself being suddenly removed to meet the Lord in the air. There are blessings in knowing the joy of "spiritually having your bags packed and ready!" This means that all your business and the details of your life are settled. Nothing is left undone. If the Lord should return at this very moment, you know there is nothing that you have been meaning to get around to addressing.

- **_The Covenant is compelling._** The marriage covenant is the pledging of your life to another. It is crucial for you to remember that Malachi calls your spouse, "Thy companion and the wife of thy covenant" (2:10).

Think of it! Pledging your life to another! When properly understood, as you pledge your life to another, it no longer belongs to you. You have given yourself to your spouse. There is no greater joy than to know that you and your spouse are reserved for each other. Neither you nor your spouse will ever find a lasting and meaningful relationship in pornography or adulterous affairs.

- **_The Word of God is cleansing._** Never has pornography been more easily accessible. With a few clicks of the mouse, it can come on the screen twenty-four hours a day. Never has it been more important that couples bring the Word of God into their marriage. Sharing the Word together brings cleansing to each life. The Psalmist said, 'Wherewithal shall a young man cleanse his way? By taking heed thereto according to Thy Word. With my whole heart have I sought Thee: O let me not wander from Thy commandments. Thy Word have I hid in mine heart, that I might not sin against Thee" (Psalm 119:9-11).

If you and your spouse want to keep your priorities straight, daily make time to read the Word and pray together. Pastor Kenward had his work cut out for him. Imagine what Les and Court's marriage would have been like if they had prayed regularly and loved unconditionally.

- **_The submission is controlling._** A wonderful blessing takes place as couples grasp the meaning of the mutual submission of Ephesians 5:21, where Paul says, "Submitting yourselves one to another in the fear of God." Think of it. You are commanded to fear God and submit yourself unto your spouse.

Being submitted to your spouse will impact everything you do and say. It is not a nagging ball and chain around your leg. Rather, it is the delightful loving tenderness that the Lord greatly desires to grow in your life. He wants you to love your spouse in ways that you never dreamed.

Go ahead and ask Him! Quietly ask the Lord to give you a love and determination to submit yourself in a dynamic, tender devotion to your spouse. You will discover sweet security as you are being kept, reserved, and controlled in doing what is right, wholesome, and righteous in your marriage.

What if these things have not been taking place? What if you and your spouse are sounding more like Les and Court? What if your ways are not pleasing to the Lord? What must you do? Keep reading!

- ***The solution is confessing.*** Healing and restoration begin at the point of honest confession. Strip away all the excuses. Do not try to minimize the sinfulness of the action. Don't trivialize what God says is sin. Confess it.

  Confession of our sin to the Lord is commanded and explained as He told us, "If we confess our sins, He is faithful and just to forgive us our sins, and to cleanse us from all unrighteousness" (1 John 1:9). To confess means to agree with Him as to the sin committed and the seriousness of that sin.

  Confessing our sin to our spouse is much wiser than being caught in our sin by our spouse. For Leslie, it would have been best never to have sinned via pornography and the affair with Allyson. But after the sin had taken place, do you see how his fracture deepened by not confessing and forsaking it? Courtney catching him in the adulterous affair furthered the fracture to the point of really making it complicated to reconcile.

Count on this being true in your marriage. Right priorities are established and demonstrated by the deliberate, intentional placing of higher value upon your spouse than what you place upon yourself. Your spouse's safety, blessing, regard, and welfare become your highest goal because of your fear of God. What power! Procrastination is overcome by understanding and implementing these simple principles of purity before the Lord.

Think about these questions

1. Do you know someone who has made poor choices in life which have escalated into sinful choices?

2. Can you see how much this has wounded the marriage?

3. Have you made sinful choices that have hurt your spouse and marriage? If so, are you procrastinating in addressing the situation?

Don't delay. Things are not just going to get better automatically on their own. The longer you wait, the more difficult the repair is going to be.

Meet Frank and Nancy who procrastinated with their finances

Frank and Nancy were a dear couple who lived what appeared to be modest lives. Their children, ages four, six, and ten were polite and well-behaved. Surely they were a model family, or so it seemed. Frank served as a deacon, and Nancy sang in the choir and served on the hospitality committee. But there was a secret Frank and Nancy shared.

"After meeting with Les and Courtney and discovering their situation, I wonder what in the world Frank and Nancy could want to talk about," Pastor Kenward thought to himself.

As he was pondering what was going on with this dear couple, he looked up and saw them pulling into the church parking lot. "I guess I will soon find out, won't I, Lord?" he whispered in prayer.

After a few moments of uneasy small talk, Frank asked the dear pastor to please open in prayer. It was a joy to pray for them and to ask the Lord for wisdom and direction regarding whatever matter they wished to discuss. Pastor could hear what he thought was muffled crying from both of the folks as he prayed. After he concluded his prayer, he assured them of his love and proceeded to ask how he could be of help to them.

"Pastor, the Lord has been bringing me under conviction as the spiritual leader of our home," Frank confessed. "In fact, I have been hit with a real wake-up call this week. We wanted to surprise you, but I guess we didn't think it through very well," Frank continued.

Nancy reached over and took his hand as Frank said, "Pastor, I had the feeling that the Lord wanted me in the ministry. I should have told you this long ago," he said as he looked up at the pastor.

"We enjoyed the speaker from the Bible college two weeks ago. I talked with him in the foyer just before he left. I told him that I was interested in going into the ministry. When he asked if I had ever talked with you about this, I told him I hadn't. When he asked if I had anything holding me back, like debt, it hit me like a ton of bricks. When I told him our financial situation, he was kind; however, he told me to make an appointment with you immediately," Frank choked out.

By this time Nancy spoke barely above a whisper as she said, "We are so in debt that the speaker told us it would be impossible for us to even entertain going to Bible college right now."

There was silence in the pastor's office for a moment. Pastor Kenward spoke quietly as he asked, "How deeply indebted are you, Frank and Nancy? It can't be that bad, can it?"

"It's bad, Pastor," Frank answered. "At first we made a few poor choices, and we talked about having to be more careful. We then started putting things on our credit card and then on another credit card, and then still another. We bought things that we couldn't afford and have gone on vacations and run up balances that we absolutely can't manage. To tell you the truth, not even counting our mortgage, we are in debt over $47,000. I can't even begin to show you the things that added up to that amount. I don't know where our money has gone. We're going to lose the house and probably Nan's car. I just can't juggle the debt collectors any longer," Frank sobbed.

"Pastor," Nancy continued, "I told Frank that we had to stop. He wanted to go to Disney one more time. I told him we needed to get help from you or a financial advisor, but Frank bought a new refrigerator, stove, and dryer and put them on a new credit card. It just doesn't stop, Pastor. He continues to buy and spend. I almost think he can't help it any longer. If we had just come to you when all this started, we wouldn't be in this terrible situation. What are we going to do now?" Nancy asked with a tone of resentment, hopelessness, and bitterness in her voice.

"Everyone thinks we're the model family," Frank said in dejection, "but actually we are the model of a family who is drowning in debt. What a model. I truly wish I had come a long time ago," Frank concluded. "If only I had taken it seriously at the start of all this. What do we do now?" Frank asked.

Don't procrastinate with wrong financial decisions and growing indebtedness

If you are plunging deeper into debt, you need to make an appointment with your pastor. Either he will help you to create a budget on which to live and a roadmap on how to get out of debt, or he will connect you with a financial ministry that can help you with this. Stop unnecessary spending. Sounds easy, doesn't it? But perhaps you and your spouse need special help to accomplish this. Get that help. Don't delay.

Think of these Biblical principles relating to your financial situation:

- ***Budgets are a wise tool to implement.*** When followed, a budget can keep you from disastrous and unwise decisions.

    "For which of you, intending to build a tower, does not sit down first and count the cost, whether he has enough to finish it—lest, after he has laid the foundation, and is not able to finish, all who see it begin to mock him, saying, This man began to build and was not able to finish" (Luke 14:28-30 NKJV).

    Your pastor or your financial advisor will help you list your income as well as your expenses. This will not be prison walls to you. Rather, this will be guardrails to help you avoid unnecessary injuries and disasters.

- ***Change the way you view your indebtedness.*** Many people in our current culture do not seem to view indebtedness as being very serious. It is not uncommon to hear people speak lightly of their deepening debt, never intending to meet their financial responsibilities. Perhaps you need to change the way you are viewing your indebtedness.

    The writer of the book of Proverbs gave very good advice to his readers. He wrote, "The rich rules over the poor, and the borrower is servant to the lender" (Proverbs 22:7).

The lender demands payment on or very near the date the bill is due each month. Typically the lender doesn't care if you are feeling well or not. The lender doesn't care if you really want to go on vacation or not. The lender wants his money back with interest. If you are going to make life changes in the areas of indebtedness, it must start with the way you view your situation. "Servant to the lender" provides the motivation to get out from under this burden.

- ***Master your money.*** The Lord Jesus clearly warned, "No one can serve two masters; for either he will hate the one and love the other, or else he will be loyal to the one and despise the other. You cannot serve God and mammon" (Matthew 6:24).

You and your spouse must come to an agreement concerning finances. Have you and your spouse ever invested time and talked about this? Have you prayed about this? Have you ever worked out a manageable budget? If you do not master your money, slowly but surely, it will master or control you.

It may surprise you how much the Bible addresses the subject of you and your money. As with all of God's Word, it is up-to-date and totally relevant in everything it addresses about money.

For instance, God's Word warns you not to co-sign a loan unless you are willing and able to pay it (Proverbs 22:26-27). If you borrow, repay every single penny (Psalm 37:21). Unwise financial decisions must be resolved as quickly as is humanly possible (Proverbs 6:1-5).

Always remember this parting financial principle: you can never, absolutely never outgive God. Be a generous and cheerful giver to the Lord (2 Corinthians 8, 9). When people get into debt, sadly one of the first things to go is financial giving and support of the local church. Be wise in your giving.

For further reading and an actual budget form, see "From This Day Forward—Preparing Couples for the Journey of a Lifetime" pages 37-39 by Dr. Michael Peck available through Regular Baptist Press (www.rbpstore.org).

Did You See the Pattern?

All of the couples who saw Pastor Kenward procrastinated when it came to fixing their problems. Just as unwise homeowners who ignored that electrical or plumbing problem when it was little and now through denial, neglect, and procrastination face a major repair, these couples denied, neglected, and procrastinated addressing their problems.

The three situations, wrong priorities, sinful choices, and financial indebtedness, are among the most commonly ignored problems that procrastinating couples face. All three typically start off small. Slowly but surely they grow. Through procrastination they are allowed to fester until the problem becomes nearly intolerable. Rather than requiring a *little* effort to restore and repair the problem early on, thanks to procrastination's, "We're going to get around to it," the little problem now has become a *big*, glaring problem.

Don't procrastinate.

Think about these questions

1. Do you or your spouse tend to procrastinate? What are some of the consequences you have witnessed as a result of this?

2. Do you and your spouse regularly talk and pray about situations that could grow larger and become more difficult? What attitudes are evident?

3. Do you or your spouse identify with any of the three couples in their areas of difficulty? If so, are you willing to discuss this with your pastor or a marriage counselor?

4. Are you and your spouse willing to work on situations before they grow into larger situations? How is this demonstrated?

"Don't Procrastinate!"

I can hear the wise pastor
as he pleads with his church family,
"Don't put off acting on God's Word.
Seek to view everything from the Lord's perspective.
If it is important to the Lord,
then it must be important to you as well.
Little things tend to become
big things before we know it.
The dripping faucet won't fix itself.
Neither will your marriage.
Be lovingly intentional.
Fix the situation today, or
face the consequences later."
With that statement the service came to a conclusion.
A very wise couple came under conviction and
determined to begin working right away on the "dripping faucet"
situation in their marriage.
A very unwise couple came under conviction and
decided to work "sooner or later" on the "dripping faucet"
situation in their marriage.
How do you suppose their response to the pastor's illustration turned out?
The wise couple was able to work on their issues rather easily and quickly.
The unwise couple put it off. Things got significantly worse, and their
problem became very difficult to fix. The lesson to be learned is
not to procrastinate.

It is my prayer that there will be a little "dust" which is the evidence that you are working in this area in your marriage. Constructing a beautiful marriage is a lot like constructing a beautiful house!

Chapter Eight
Enjoying the Seasons

Keep Looking Forward to Eternity

"To everything there is a season, and a time to every purpose under the heaven: A time to be born, and a time to die; a time to plant, and a time to pluck up that which is planted" (Ecclesiastes 3:1-2)

"But I trusted in Thee, O LORD: I said,
Thou art my God. My times are in Thy hands (Psalm 31:15)
Seasons ever change.
While time never stands still,
may the Lord grant you enjoyment in
the season through which you are traveling.
Christ walks with you and your dear spouse on this
amazing journey of a lifetime.
There is help for the difficult times
and joy for the hard as well as the happy days
in each of the seasons.

Remember Grandpa's note: Enjoy the Seasons. Always Keep Looking Forward to Eternity.

Key thought: *In Genesis 8, God promised Noah that the seasons would continue as long as the earth exists. Regardless of where you live, spring, summer, fall, and winter bring variety and change. Likewise, into your life and marriage seasons will come and go. It is so important to understand the seasons and to enjoy them with your spouse. Make rich the seasons of your life and marriage.*

Tim and Kirsten, who you met in the beginning chapters of the book, were enjoying the young couples in their Sunday school class. Reluctant at first to teach this class because the "young couples" were so much younger than Kirsten and him, Tim thanked the Lord every day for the many blessings that had come to them through this Sunday school class. They loved being with the younger couples. Likewise, the younger couples were so encouraged by the Mitchell's consistent walk with the Lord and by their marriage. It was obvious that Tim and Kirsten loved the Lord and truly loved each other as well.

One of the couples with whom Tim and Kirsten enjoyed friendship was Ken and Alisha. Chatting during a breakfast fellowship before Sunday school started, Ken and Tim were talking about the sudden onset of winter.

"It feels like we jumped over fall this year and headed right into winter," Ken said. "When we talked with your dad and uncles as they built our house, I remember one of them talking about your grandfather. They often referred to some of the things that he would say or write to people. He told us that your grandpa often told folks to enjoy the changing seasons in their new houses."

Tim smiled. "That's my grandpa. He is now with the Lord, Ken, but I can still hear him telling folks how much he loved the various seasons. If he was asked what his favorite season is, he would always tell folks that it was the one we were in right now. I wish you could have met him, Ken. What a Godly man. He loved the Lord and his family, and oh, did my grandpa ever love my grandma," Tim spoke softly. He reminisced with gladness and admiration about happy times with his grandparents, and it was obvious to Ken that Tim missed them terribly and viewed them very fondly.

"Speaking of my grandpa, when Kirsten and I were engaged, I remember that there was a family in the church I used to attend that I thought was really living for the Lord. Then suddenly they made an announcement that they were divorcing. I was shattered, Ken, and to tell you the truth, I was scared. If divorce could happen to that family, I was afraid it could happen to Kirsten and me. With that heartache being so fresh, the next time I had lunch with my grandparents, I asked them the secret to the success of their marriage.

"Of all things, my grandpa wrote me a note about how he builds houses and said that if Kirsten and I would build our marriage in the same way, we could have a beautiful marriage," Tim said as he drank his coffee.

Ken listened intently and thought about Tim's statement. It made a profound impact upon his life. Mitchell and Sons Construction was known for the beautiful homes and outstanding Christian testimony.

"They certainly built a beautiful house for us," Ken thoughtfully said to Tim. "I can definitely see that there were several correlations between the building of our house and the building of our marriage. In fact, your Uncle Hank often spoke to us about our house as they were building it, and he sometimes spoke about our marriage that we are building. We really needed that, Tim, and certainly we appreciated it. Often Alisha and I would talk about the blessing of having a Godly builder for our house who encouraged us in our marriage," Ken said with sincerity.

Tim smiled as he said, "It reminded me of Grandpa's note when you spoke about the house my uncles built and the changing seasons coming so quickly. The last thing on the note that my grandpa gave me actually said something about the seasons, I think. I'm pretty sure he said something about enjoying them. It has been a while since I read Grandpa's note, but I'm pretty sure the seasons were the last thing. Now my curiosity is up. When I get home today, I'm going to get that note out. I haven't looked at it in a long time. I want to see exactly what Grandpa said about the seasons.

"Anyway, I have to ask you, Ken, are you enjoying your new home? I hope everything is working out well for you and Alisha," Tim continued.

"We couldn't be happier. And about the seasons, we really are enjoying the changing seasons in our new home. I would hardly have known it was fall except that the wind blows our neighbor's leaves into our yard. It makes us feel like we already have mature trees," Ken laughed as he fooled with Tim.

It was a great service at church that morning. As Kirsten, Tim, and their family returned home, Tim said, "Honey, I will be glad to help set the table, but there is something I want to do first. It will only take a second.

Enjoying the Seasons

Ken and I were speaking about my grandfather this morning, and I want to check something he wrote on his note to us."

"Take your time," Kirsten called back. "I'm just starting the carrots."

Tim went to the place where the special note was carefully tucked away. Gently unfolding it, there, in the personal handwriting of his beloved grandfather, was the note that Tim and Kirsten had cherished for a long time:

"Tim, here are the things I always talk to couples about as they get ready to build their new home. If you and Kirsten will do the same things in your marriage, then you will be best friends even when the honeymoon's over. Here is what I tell folks who want a house.

> *Remember these seven things:*
>
> *First, you have to think about the design of it. What kind of house do you want?*
>
> *Second, you have to follow the architectural plans.*
>
> *Third, you need to build upon a good solid foundation.*
>
> *Fourth, as the house is built, it stands empty and will echo, so you need to furnish it and decorate it.*
>
> *Fifth, over the years you need to watch out for anything that will harm the structure of your house. I always tell folks around this part of the country that they need to keep their eyes open for tornadoes, thieves, and termites!*
>
> *Sixth, you need to keep repairing things when they break down. I tell folks not to procrastinate. If something breaks, fix it right away when it is little!*
>
> *Last, you just plain simply need to enjoy the seasons that will come as a homeowner.*

This is how I build beautiful houses. This is the same formula that your grandmother and I used to build a beautiful marriage. Always remember how much your grandmother and I love you and Kirsten. Take no shortcuts. Seek the Lord daily. Build your marriage like I build houses. Grandpa"

"He did indeed talk about seasons and enjoying them!" Tim said to Kirsten as they and their children prepared for lunch together. He went on to explain more about his conversation with Ken during breakfast fellowship. "I really am enjoying the seasons that we are sharing together, Honey," Tim said to his dear wife as he hugged her and kissed her cheek.

"And I am enjoying them with you as well, Mr. Timothy Mitchell," Kirsten said with a smile. "Though we don't know what is ahead, it is so special to understand that the Lord has planned all our seasons. You and I can always ask the Lord to help us to discover enjoyment in the season we are in," Kirsten concluded.

What a great statement Kirsten made that day. You don't know what is ahead, but it is tremendous to understand that the Lord, Who created the coming and going of seasons, wants to help you by walking through the present season with you and your spouse.

Everything in life has its season. A season is that period of time in which particular life circumstances or features take place. Spring is often associated with the time of beginnings. Summer is associated with warm weather and fun vacations taken together. With the arrival of fall, the weather begins to turn cooler, sweatshirts are pulled up out of storage, and falling leaves keep homeowners busy. For those who live in the colder climate, the days of fall soon turn cold, and winter arrives. To some, winter is a fun time of outdoor sports activity; however, to many folks, winter is a difficult season of time as the cold winds blow. Winter requires a great deal of carefulness for people to navigate. Even with its challenges, winter can be a wonderful time and the season enjoyed.

Think of how striking the similarities are between your marriage and the ever-changing seasons in the natural world around you. Your marriage will certainly go through various seasons. If you are to stay best friends with your spouse, it will be important for you to understand the seasons and see how the Lord wants to help you and your spouse enjoy them.

The Springtime Season of Your Marriage
Engagement and the First Five Years

The Season of Discovery and Adjustment

What a special season. This is an exciting time of life. You have discovered the person with whom you want to live the rest of your lifetime. Whether you are beginning the engagement process or have been married a few years, you need to make this very precious season a great start to your lifetime. Think of the foundational principles that must be established in creating a Godly and lasting marriage.

Good questions for engaged and newlywed couples

Your engagement period and the first five years should be such a special time in your life. You are beginning a journey. It is the "the journey of a lifetime." Marriage really is a journey that takes a lifetime to complete. No wise person begins a lengthy journey without good preparations. Only running a quick errand can be done without much planning (probably even quick errands would go better with a little bit of preparation!) Certainly long journeys require good directions, adequate finances, bags packed properly, and much, much more.

The Old Testament prophet Amos posed a question that has lasted for generations. Think about what he asked. "Can two walk together, except they be agreed?" (Amos 3:3).

Based on that question, here are several key principles that are very important as you begin your marriage journey. To really enjoy this season, you must formulate your understanding as well as come to understand your spouse's point of view in these key areas. These questions are designed to help you enjoy this springtime of your marriage. The more you and your spouse understand each other's opinions, preferences and even convictions, the better your marriage will be.

Get the most of these questions

This resource provides you with key questions to think about and discuss with your fiancé or newly married partner. To receive the most help, both should be agreed to do this. Both must see the value (sometimes men are not as quick to see the value at first!) Select a time that is good for both of you. Don't rush through them. Some questions will be answered within a moment or two. Others will take some time to work through. It will be interesting to see how many times you already agree on an answer. It will always be important to consider the answers and opinions of your spouse. If you cannot come to compromise and agreement, be sure to discuss this with your pastor or marriage counselor at the appropriate time.

Personal questions that require thought and attention

These questions will be written as if you are not yet married. Please adapt them to your marriage situation.

- Why do you want to marry me?
- What are the strengths and weaknesses of our lives? How do these complement each other?
- When disagreements and conflicts arise in our marriage, how will we resolve them?
- Have we talked through and reached an agreement as to whether we should rent or purchase our home and how much of our income should be spent on housing?
- Do we agree on the need for a budget, and have we tried to project our expenses? Read the article at www.michaelpeck.org: "Marriage, Engaged Couples: We Can't Live on Love Alone—Our Financial Situation."
- Do we really understand what a healthy sexual relationship looks like?
- How many children would we like to have someday? How long should we wait before we try to get pregnant?
- Have we settled on birth control, and have we worked through this with our physician to guarantee our chosen method prevents conception and does not function as an abortion which terminates our pregnancy?
- How will a baby change our lives?

Spiritual questions that require thought and attention
- Are we seriously praying about our relationship with each other and with the Lord?
- What place does the Lord Jesus have in our personal lives and our lives together as a couple?
- Do we both know the Lord Jesus in a personal way as our own Savior?
- What place does worship have in our time together as a couple? Are we satisfied with how often we read the Bible and pray together?
- Are we in agreement as to which church we will attend, how often we will attend it, in what ways we will serve and how much we will financially support it?

Financial questions that require thought and attention
- As we view each other, how would you describe my view of money? Is money too important to me? Is it not important enough? Would you say that I have the right view of finances and am helping you to manage your finances wisely?
- Have we settled on whether we will have separate accounts or joint accounts?
- What are three or four things that we would like to acquire someday for which we must save?
- What is our view of indebtedness? How much is too much? How many credit cards should we have, and what is our view of paying each card off at the end of the month?
- What percentage of our income should we have for savings and investment?

Practical questions that require thought and attention
- As we look at the marriages of our parents, what are several good things we would like to incorporate into our marriage? What are several things that we would not incorporate?
- Who is going to pay the bills and keep the checkbook?
- Who is going to do the cooking? How will we share the household chores such as cleaning, washing the clothes, grocery shopping, etc.?

- How often should we eat out, spend time with friends, or reserve a night at home where we can enjoy being together? What are some things we can do that both of us really enjoy?
- What are some safeguards we are establishing to keep our marriage strong and healthy? Are we open and honest with each other? Are we both satisfied with our level of communication? Do we demonstrate that we really care about each other? Are we really connecting? Does the Lord Jesus have first place priority in our personal lives and marriage plans?

Enjoy this season

The main lesson for this season is to enjoy the discoveries. You will discover many things about your spouse, about yourself, and about your marriage. Don't let anything rob you of the joy of this season of your life. This truly is a once-in-a-lifetime experience.

- *A time of new beginnings.* Your engagement and the first five years are special times of beginnings. You are beginning your journey together. You are beginning in your new house or apartment. You may be in the beginning of your career. You are beginning new routines. You are beginning a brand new experience. You are beginning to get to know each other in very special ways.

- *Settle these questions and be willing to compromise.* You can enjoy this season of your marriage by reviewing the questions and resolving any kind of disagreement with your spouse. Determine that you will not be stubborn and insist on your own way. Seek the Lord together. Lovingly talk with your spouse about your point of view on these questions.

- *Lifelong patterns getting started.* Lifelong patterns will be planted and established in this season. While it is possible to make changes in any season, this is the season of commencement. This is the period of time when you and your beloved prepare to begin your journey of a lifetime together and to let the whole world know that you are reserved for each other.

Here the patterns of how you work together in household chores, manage the finances, determine work strategies, raise the children that will come to you, manage the time you have for the Lord and each other, as well as worship habits and convictions relating to spiritual things are established for your home and family.

Dennis and Jan grew up together and became high school sweethearts. Both were good communicators, and both seemed to think alike and even share similar interests. When they became engaged, Dennis insisted that he didn't see the need for premarital counseling. "After all," he said to her, "we're not like other couples. We've known each other forever. There's nothing more for you to discover about how I think and believe. The rest we can settle after the wedding."

Jan was thoughtful about his opinion, but she wasn't very comfortable about it. Even after explaining how important she felt the premarital counseling was, he still doubted the need. Wisely their pastor challenged them to work through the questions you have been reviewing. Dennis was shocked. They couldn't be further apart in their responses.

Fortunately Dennis and Jan had wonderful success in their premarital counseling. "Pastor Kenward," Dennis said, "at first I thought this wasn't necessary for us. I soon learned that we had a lot of talking to do and coming to agreement in our marriage. Thank you for taking all the time with us and making such an investment in our marriage," Dennis concluded.

It can be the same for you. Talk through these questions. Come to agreement. Seek the Lord and His blessing. Enjoy this season!

The Summertime Season of Your Marriage
From Five to Twenty or Twenty-five Years Together

Buckle Up for Some of the Busiest Times of Your Lives

What a special season. This is an amazing time of life. If the Lord has given you children, then you are traveling through the daily adjustments of it no longer being just "you and me." It is now the season of "us". Sometimes it may seem more like it is a season of "them" because children require so much time, investment, and sharing.

How is this going for you and your spouse? How is it really going?

It is so very busy all the time
It feels like it is the busiest of all the seasons. You are becoming busier with your work. More and more demands are being made on your time, and now the Lord is bringing children into your lives. From the moment these precious children arrive, life will never be the same. It is wonderful, but it is never the same. There are appointments to be kept, homework to be completed, school functions to attend, doctors' visits, dental and vision appointments, church activities, and a host of other things that clamor for your attention.

Have you ever watched jugglers spinning plates on extended poles? The juggler has to keep each plate spinning fast enough to keep it from falling. Running from plate to plate, it eventually becomes impossible to keep every plate spinning and results in quite a crash! Does that sound like your life right now?

Consider these marriage commandments
Being busy with "good" things can rob you of the time for the "excellent" things. How busy are you and your family? Have you at times thought that you were getting overbooked? Think about these important commandments, look up the references, and plan a strategy with your spouse to implement them. They will help you enjoy this season of your life and marriage.

- *Honoring.* Thou shalt honor the Lord your God by loving Him first. The Lord Jesus said "Thou shalt love the Lord thy God with all thy heart and with all thy soul and with all thy mind (Matthew 22:37).

    It is hard to explain but true nevertheless. Loving the Lord and honoring Him is the starting point of bringing every other aspect of your life and marriage into right priorities.

- *Scheduling.* Thou shalt seek to wisely manage your schedule. Do not overload it to the point of being unwise (James 1:5).

Fortunately, most believers are not acting wickedly and scheduling unrighteous activities. However, some believers do schedule too many good things in a typical week that can make a vibrant marriage with quality time nearly impossible. Many good things unwisely scheduled take time away from excellent things.

- ***Worshipping.*** Thou shalt remember to seek the Lord daily, to worship Him and to ask for His wisdom, direction and strength for the day (Psalm 63:1-2, 8).

It is sad to know that more than a few believing families seldom or never worship together during the week. Worship is the recognition of the worthiness of your great God. It is the expression of joy and devotion before Him and the acknowledgement of your great need of the Lord and His blessings.

Now imagine telling the Lord, "I'm glad to belong to You, Lord, but I'm very sorry. My family and I are too busy for You right now. But we'll check back with You so we can get You scheduled. Surely there will be a few minutes in our schedule in several weeks or so!"

No one would tell the Lord this in words, but many families tell Him this in actions. Dad really needs to step it up in his spiritual leadership, and Mom really needs to support Dad's efforts in leading his family. Your marriage will be blessed, and you will be spiritually strengthened as you take even a few minutes each day to lead your family in worship.

- ***Loving.*** Thou shalt not only love your mate, thou shalt tell your mate often of your love and then demonstrate it.

"But God commendeth His love toward us, in that, while we were yet sinners, Christ died for us" (Romans 5:8). The word "commendeth" is *synistemi* which gives the idea of "showing, exhibiting, or demonstrating." Don't keep your love the best kept secret in town! Show your love to your spouse.

Think about these questions

1. How does our spouse know of your love?

2. When was the last the time you intentionally demonstrated your love for your spouse? Did your spouse recognize it?

- ***Connecting.*** Thou shalt take time to physically connect with your spouse. "My beloved is mine, and I am his" (Song of Solomon 2:16).

Growing closer to your spouse results in the joy of being reserved for another. It is the affectionate joy of the husband and wife who are deeply in love. How do you express this and grow in this blessing? Among other things, linger in the embrace, kiss with more than a glancing blow, hold your mate's hand, snuggle closely and touch your spouse with the touch of tenderness.

- ***Caring.*** Thou shalt show your interest in the life and day's events of your mate. This is connecting emotionally with your spouse because you genuinely care. Give your loved one undivided attention as you listen, and show that you care.

"This is my beloved, and this is my friend, O daughters of Jerusalem (Song of Solomon 5:16). Not only was her spouse the love of her life, he was also her friend. This speaks of the emotional connection they enjoyed as they shared the commonality and fellowship of their marriage.

This is the goal of the marriage construction that you and your spouse are working on. Staying best friends long after the honeymoon's over is much more than just a title. It is the joy of a vibrant marriage.

- ***Modeling.*** Thou shalt seek to be good examples of the tremendous love Christ has for the church and the kind of respect the church has for Christ (Ephesians 5:22-33).

Paul certainly had cause to rejoice in the wonderful love for the church that Christ demonstrates. He truly had good reason to remind the church that believers should be deeply struck with awe and respect for the Lord, but he had more in mind than just that truth.

He wrote to demonstrate the principles of a deeply intimate marriage that thrives on love and respect. Just as Christ loves with sacrificial love that holds nothing back and as the church deeply respects the Lord, so should the Godly husband and wife be to the other.

- *Prioritizing.* Thou shalt put your mate above yourself and seek to make your spouse the higher priority. "Let each esteem other better than themselves" (Philippians 2:3).

What a wonderful plan the Lord has for the Godly believer. Avoid the trap of selfishness and self-centeredness. This command based on Paul's writing to the church at Philippi helps you to learn how to hold your mate (and others!) in a much higher priority than yourself.

- *Glorifying.* Thou shalt seek to glorify God in your home and marriage. "Whatsoever you do, do all to the glory of God (1 Corinthians 10:31).

What a great goal. In every area of your home and marriage, Christ can be honored and glorified or He can be dishonored and disrespected. Can you begin to imagine the blessings that can come to your marriage if you and your spouse deliberately determine that glorifying the Lord Jesus in every area of your marriage will be your goal?

- *Asking.* Thou shalt call upon the Lord and ask Him to bless your mate and your marriage. "Call unto me, and I will answer thee and show thee great and mighty things which thou knowest not" (Jeremiah 33:3).

Earlier we thought about family worship. This is the time that you and your spouse together invest with the Lord. Many couples are experiencing blessings that they never dreamed possible directly related to beginning to pray together. Hearing your spouse praying for you, thanking the Lord for bringing you to her or him, and asking God to bless you brings such a deep and tender love. If you and your spouse are not praying together each day, you are missing such a blessing.

Happiness and successful marriages don't happen by making "thou shalt" lists. Marriages are much more than just a list of details to check off and then forget. These are Biblical principles that our great God has given in His design for Godly and gracious living. When these principles are intentionally and consistently implemented, wonderful blessings will take place.

Think of what happened to Alan and Candi. These dear folks were married soon after high school. Candi dropped out of community college because their first child was on the way after a little over two years of their marriage. Though they were thrilled, they honestly admitted later that they were actually still getting to know each other when Markie came! Following Markie, Sammy, Peter, Luke, and Marcy made their grand appearances.

Both parents gave great thanks to the Lord for their precious family. For years they hardly took time to sit and talk. By the end of their typical day, both were so exhausted, they quickly kissed good-night, prayed a rushed and exhausted prayer, and fell off to sleep. Alan worked ten hours a day. Both found themselves rushing to church or school activities, running errands, keeping up with doctors' appointments, getting braces for two of the children, sporting events, and listening to piano recitals (which sounded a lot better than the piano practices!).

The years started flying by. Alan and Candi felt like some of the busiest people in the world! They had invested a lot of time and energy into their children. Fortunately they became convicted of their priorities and started to creatively make time for each other so that they could continue to build a strong marriage. In spite of many children, a full schedule of activities, and lots going on, they determined not to neglect their marriage.

They knew that they wanted a strong marriage and also greatly desired to build a strong family. Ultimately, they gave the Lord the right priority. They consistently asked the Lord to have the first place in their lives. They consistently read the Word of God and asked the Lord to help them implement what they read.

They invested by giving their marriage the right priority. Together they managed their schedules to keep from becoming overly busy. They enjoyed reconnecting every evening and shared quality time together.

Enjoying the Seasons

They joyfully gave their family the right priority. Family Bible reading was a time that everyone looked forward to. Family game night became a great tradition. Fun times such as all the guys preparing an evening meal, family camping trips, Dad's famous, "You'll never guess where we're going this time" became family building adventures. This equipped their children to grow and mature.

The day would come when their children would marry and have children. Each would think back to their parents' example. A second generation of believers discovered that you can be busy but still love the Lord, love each other, and love your family.

Does this sound like you and your spouse in this season?

Think about these questions

1. What are you and your spouse doing to intentionally create special times to invest in your marriage?

2. What are several challenges that you and your spouse are facing in this season of your life and marriage?

3. When was the last time you and your spouse went on a date, had couple's devotions together, or reserved an evening just to be together?

4. Are you and your spouse enjoying this season of your marriage?

The Fall Season of Your Marriage As the Nest Starts to Empty

How Fast Our Children Grew Up! Where Did the Time Go?

What a special season this is! It certainly is true that children change everything. At your child's high school graduation party, did you say to your friends, "I can't believe how quickly the years have gone by! It seems like only yesterday that we were beginning with kindergarten, and here we are today at high school graduation"? Then before you knew it, you were celebrating college graduation!

Time does have a way of flying. All too soon your children have grown up. The time comes when they move out, (or at least for longer periods of time), and you are officially empty-nesters!

How is this going for you and your spouse?

Still concerned but enjoying the freedom

This can be a special period of time for you and your spouse. It certainly will be an adjustment as you watch the last of your children take flight. This doesn't mean that you are done being concerned for them and helping when the opportunity lends itself, even giving advice, if they ask. But it does mean that you have much more freedom from the daily "hands-on" responsibilities of parenting. You now have much more time to enjoy the great blessings in your marriage as empty-nesters.

Even couples with large families and demanding schedules can invest in their marriage and discover the joy of returning to the empty nest. You started your marriage with just the two of you; now it is just the two of you once again. This adjustment might include times of loneliness and a feeling of emptiness. Where once parents were kept busy with all the responsibilities, now there are open periods of time on the calendar. Some find it a difficult adjustment; however, this can be a wonderful season of life to enjoy with your spouse.

Here are several things to do that will help you enjoy this season.

Special time to grow closer to the Lord

This can be a tremendous time of really getting to know the Lord in a deeper and greater way. As a couple you can make it a priority to learn more about the Lord together.

After the Apostle Paul met the Lord on the road to Damascus (Acts 9:1-6), he wasn't satisfied to just know that he was saved. He wanted to grow in his knowledge of his great and awesome God. He told the believers in Philippi, "That I may know Him, and the power of His resurrection, and the fellowship of His sufferings, being made conformable unto His death" (Philippians 3:10). He wanted to know the Lord in a deeper and more intimate way.

Is this a goal for you and your spouse? The key to experiencing a lasting friendship with your spouse is for you as a couple to grow in your knowledge and love for the Lord. How do you do this? One way is by using a personal journal (or compiling a journal together) to record notes from your Bible reading about Who the Lord Jesus is, what He did, and what He says that speaks to you personally.

Make it personal. Do not view Him as some very distant God who is far removed from you and your marriage. Rather, view Him as One Who deeply loves you and cares about you and your marriage. View Him as the loving Partner in your marriage Who wants to bless and guide your marriage and home every day. If you know Him as your Savior, then He must be viewed as the precious One Who loves you deeply and dwells with you. Welcome Him into every part of your day. These should be days that the Lord Jesus can become more real to you than ever.

Develop a consistent devotional life
Children bring tremendous activity into the schedule of every married couple. There were activities with the children at church, school, and within your own household. Now your children are grown. You are still busy, but it is not the same as it was when your children were growing up. Didn't it seem like your time had demands from every direction screaming for your attention? Now your schedule affords the time to develop a consistent devotional time with the Lord.

The Lord Jesus wants to become even more precious to you. Spend time with Him. Look forward to reading your Bible and praying. Pray by yourself at times. Include special times of prayer with your spouse.

Discuss as a couple what time of day will work best for your devotions together. Look forward to this time, and enjoy holding hands and talking with your Heavenly Father. Pray out loud for each other as well as your family. This will be a precious time, well invested as you seek the Lord (Jeremiah 33:3).

Keep your marriage fresh
Though you are growing older, you do not have to grow boring and stale. Though your body may not have as much energy as it used to, don't

vegetate. Beware that your marriage doesn't drift into being the same old thing day in and day out.

Your spouse is your special companion. Malachi wrote, "Yet she is thy companion, and the wife of thy covenant (Malachi 2:14). We have written about this earlier, but think about it. This means that your spouse is the one who is accompanying you on the journey of a lifetime. You are making your way together. Here are a few things that many couples in this season of life have discovered to help keep their marriage vibrant and enjoyable.

- *Worshipping.* Worship regularly with God's people. If you haven't been consistent in assembling with God's people, now is really the time to begin. You need to experience the fellowship of God's people. The folks at your local church also need your fellowship.

The Apostle Paul described this as the functioning of the body (1 Corinthians 12). You are a particular member in the body with a very specific contribution to the overall working of the body. If you haven't been active in your local church, now is the time to make this decision. If you have been faithful and active in your local ministry, don't slack off by assuming that you have nothing to contribute to the work.

- *Dating.* Date weekly. Bring variety into your weekly date. Take turns being responsible for selecting the activity and place. It doesn't have to be expensive. It doesn't have to burdensome. Dating regularly communicates that your marriage is important, your spouse is special, and the time you share together is priceless.

- *Serving.* Serve the Lord together. If at all possible, find a ministry in which you both can serve. If that is not possible, serve in whatever way the Lord wants you to in your local church and other worthwhile community opportunities. Serving will add so much to your marriage and keep it fresh. You and your spouse will find joy as you prepare for your ministry, pray for your ministry, talk about your ministry, and watch the Lord bless your ministry.

- ***Inviting.*** Be social. Invite friends to come to your house for fun and fellowship. Don't become hermits! Extend yourselves. While your children were growing up, it is possible that you made the excuse, "We don't have time. Our children are keeping us too busy." Well, now that the children are grown and have flown from your home, invite folks over. Be friendly! Talk with other couples. Share your home and your time with others.

Don't lose the joy of intimacy

Intimacy is that close emotional connection that enjoys expressing itself in the physical connection of sexuality. How wise and kind our great Creator God is! He created man and woman to find that ultimate fulfillment in full openness, closeness, and connection that comes in being one flesh.

Please allow me to be really candid with you. When you were younger and your passion was stronger, how many times when you and your spouse were enjoying marital intimacy were you suddenly interrupted at the worst moment with a knock on your bedroom door and a little voice right outside saying, "Mommy, I'm thirsty"? Many couples have experienced "the grand interruption" more than once. You may have even dreamed of the day when your children would never interrupt those special moments again!

Now that the children are grown and flown, wouldn't you think that passion would take place even more often? The interruptions are gone, so what has happened?

Pastors sit across the desk in the counseling center as one of the spouses usually looks down and says something like, "Pastor, this is awfully hard for me to talk about, but my spouse just isn't interested any more in sex. The kids are gone, and I had hoped that the frequency of our special times would increase. Now if we 'do it' once every couple of months, that's good. What is wrong with us?" Does this sound like it might fit your empty-nest home?

- ***The aging process.*** Sometimes passion or the desire to have sexual intercourse with your marriage partner wanes at this stage of the marriage. There can be several reasons for this. The aging process often makes it difficult for many men to physically function and may cause the loss of libido for many ladies. You are not alone. Do not think that this is limited exclusively to you. Sometimes surgery or physical illness make the physical act of intercourse difficult as well.

These situations really can be addressed by your primary care physician or your obstetrician/gynecologist. Please do not withdraw from your spouse if you are having problems. When a physical situation is involved, your doctor can offer good help to you. Please do not allow embarrassment to keep you from obtaining sound medical help. You and your spouse can enjoy being intimate even in this stage of life.

- *Sometimes it's resentment.* Sometimes the loss of intimacy is not a physical problem. Resentment from past misunderstandings or hurts building up over the years can cause walls to be built up. These push couples apart, and a really meaningful sexual relationship can be damaged. Sometimes wives withhold themselves as a form of revenge or punishment for their husbands' failures. Sometimes men withhold themselves as a form of resentment or pouting over offenses committed by their wives.

- *Sometimes it's sin.* Sinful acts, such as viewing pornography, instead of making sexual expression more appealing, have just the opposite results. Devastation and disappointment are the two key results of such sin. Occasionally sexual activity is withheld because of an involvement the spouse is having with someone else. While this may not be the typical situation, it does happen nonetheless.

- *Sometimes it's embarrassment.* Needless to say that most folks never had the body of a model. Somehow as the years go by, most bodies do not get better. Sometimes intimacy is lost due to embarrassment. The weight gain, stretch marks, surgical scars, or other physical situations sometimes cause a decrease in sexual desires.

- *Sometimes it's disconnect.* When the cause for loss of marital intimacy is sinful, then confession and restoration need to take place (1 John 1:9). Be honest with each other. Talk with each other. Acknowledge the "distance and disconnection" that you both sense. Seek forgiveness. Extend forgiveness. Accept the joy of forgiveness. These will be

Enjoying the Seasons

the first steps back to each other. It may have taken years for you and your spouse to get into this emotionally distant situation. It will take time to reconnect and grow closer on your journey of a lifetime. It can be done, and you will be glad you took the time and effort.

- ***The difference between sex and intimacy.*** In addition to everything we have briefly addressed about intimacy, please understand a great truth about this vital ingredient. There is a big difference between the physical act of sexuality and the emotional connection of intimacy.

Did you know that it is possible to have sex with your spouse but not really achieve intimacy? And did you know that even if you cannot physically function in the sexual act, you can still enjoy intimacy? Sexuality can deteriorate to the state where it is only a physical act. Intimacy, on the other hand, is an emotional connection that finds joy in growing closer together. It is the intentional little bridges that husband and wife build throughout the day, causing a connection emotionally that results in a precious intimacy. Even if you have undergone numerous surgeries, have physical challenges, and are not getting any younger, you can still be intimate with your spouse.

What a great time to intentionally reconnect

As you empty-nest with your spouse, you can have a wonderful time of growing closer. Sometimes couples do not even sense how distant they have grown. Just how deeply connected emotionally are you to your spouse? Have you ever talked about your connection with your spouse? Obviously you will not walk up to your spouse and say, "Are you connected to me?"

One of the great blessings of having a devotional time to read the Bible and pray with your spouse is that it lends itself to communication. Praying that you and your spouse will grow together is a wonderful prayer. Talk about your marriage with your spouse. Be deliberate and do things that will reach out to your spouse and strengthen your marriage.

Develop a thankful heart that expresses appreciation. When you are apart, keep your spouse foremost on your mind. Send a text, an email, or make a phone call touching base throughout the day, even if it is very brief. If romance is dead, pray for a miracle to bring it back to life! Hold hands, hug, kiss, and snuggle. Being close emotionally is demonstrated by the desire you and your spouse have to be close physically.

Bill and his dear wife, Louise, celebrated their fifty-fifth wedding anniversary. They attended a marriage conference at their local church with about thirty other couples, most of whom were in their twenties or thirties. During one of the coffee breaks, the speaker of the conference noticed that they were holding hands when walking to the table where donuts were available.

After introducing himself, the speaker thanked them for coming, asked how long they had been married, and made the following comment, "I noticed that you folks were holding hands. You seem to be very happy. What's the secret of your happiness?"

Bill answered, "Well preacher, we figured that we were doing pretty good in the marriage department, so we wanted to encourage the younger folks to work at their marriages. What's our secret? I would say that we talk to the Lord together, we love to be in the Word of God, we don't go to bed mad at each other, we hug a lot, and well, let's just say that even though things physically don't work as good as they once did, we still keep things romantically fresh!"

Louise gasped and swatted her husband saying, "Bill, you don't have to tell him everything!"

The marriage conference speaker had to begin the next session, but he never forgot Bill and Louise and their "keeping things romantically fresh even though things don't work so well physically."

You and your spouse can still find each other's bodies appealing and exciting, even if they "aren't what they used to be!" You and your spouse can become even better friends, and you can learn to cherish the relationship you have. Your spouse should hear you often sharing your love by your words and actions. You simply love being with each other.

These are intentional things that should become second nature through time and practice.

Enjoying the Seasons

Finally it's time to be friends with your children

Throughout your years of parenting, you were reminded over and over to 'be the parent not the friend' of your children. You probably heard your pastor preach, "Your children have plenty of friends. They need you to be the parent." You knew that powerful statement was true, so you parented. You took the hard stands. You loved your child even when there was tremendous resistance and pressures. You disciplined. You encouraged. You taught. You stayed up all night when your child was sick. You guided your child. You held fast and said, "No!" when your child wanted to do something that you knew would be unwise. Perhaps you had the heart-wrenching situation where your child screamed, "I hate you!" At times you wondered if the time would ever come that your children would at least like you!

The good news is that finally the time has come when you should actually function less as the parent and more of the friend to your children. Your child will still probably ask for your advice. They might even ask for some financial help sometime. But now the time has arrived that your child should rely on you less and less in the parenting department. Amazingly, you will discover that your concern as the parent won't lessen. You will still be concerned for your children regardless of their ages, but this is a really great time to enjoy the friendships of your children. They should be looking to you and your spouse as those with whom they would like to spend time, have lunch, do something fun, and even become friends!

Make each day count

This is not meant to be morbid, but it must be said. Be honest with yourself. You do not know how many more days the Lord will give you. Make these months and years really count for the Lord.

Moses had such insight and wisdom when he wrote, "So teach us to number our days, that we may apply our hearts unto wisdom" (Psalm 90:12). This stage of your life is a great time to live with growing appreciation to the Lord for all that He has done for you, as well as all that He wants to do in and through you in the years ahead.

Empty-nesting is a time of adjustment. Some find relief that their children have grown and flown; others find it to be a tad more on the melancholy side as the house has grown quiet, and the bedrooms are unused.

- ***Look on the blessed side of life.*** Our Lord has promised to provide everything that you need (Philippians 4:19). He will enable you to adjust to this time (Philippians 4:13). He wants to give you His peace (John 14:27; 16:33). His joy is a fruit that He wants to grow in your life (Galatians 5:22-23). Laughter doesn't have to leave your home just because you are an empty-nester. In fact, laughter is good for you and your spouse (Proverbs 17:17). Before you know it, perhaps sooner than you expect, you will have the joy of becoming a grandparent. Yes, grandchildren are a joy (Proverbs 17:6).

When you think about it, empty-nesting really never fully happens for believing spouses. The Lord, your spouse, and you can have wonderful days ahead with your grown children, their children, and your friends.

Think about these questions

1. Can you think of two or three blessings that the Lord has brought into your life and marriage in this season of life?

2. What are you doing to get to know your spouse better in this season?

3. If you could select a verse of Scripture to describe your marriage in this season, what would it be?

The Wintertime Season of Marriage
The "Senior Years"

Life is Getting Harder but Grandchildren are Wonderful

What a special season. Think of it! You are married to someone old enough to be a grandparent!

Perhaps you and your spouse never had children. For our purposes we are going to refer to this season of your marriage as the season of being a grandparent. When you were a child, probably you enjoyed visiting your grandparents. Now you are one!

Aren't grandchildren wonderful? "Children's children are the crown of old men" (Proverbs 17:6). Old men's crown! Grandpa and Grandma, you are a crowned king or queen. Perhaps you have had the experience of having one of your grandchildren innocently and sincerely ask you, "Are you old?" While you may or may not feel old, this season of life and marriage does bring you back to the reality check that there are more years behind you than ahead of you.

This doesn't have to be a sad and morbid time of life. It can be a wonderful time of relying on each other in practical ways and trusting the Lord in very pointed ways. When you were younger, you had much more energy and strength but not so much experience which leads to wisdom. Now you have much more experience which leads to wisdom but not so much strength. What an incredible season to be in!

Winters in Northern America are cold. Those who live near the Great Lakes understand the dynamics of winter. The snows come, the ice builds up, the gale winds blow, and life generally becomes more difficult in the winter. Walking can become treacherous, and driving becomes dangerous at times. Those who drive recklessly and those who walk carelessly soon find themselves in a world of trouble.

Wintertime drivers who act like it is summertime are foolish folks indeed. Wintertime driving brings a whole new set of demands and cautions to enable drivers and those around them to make their way safely. Stop and think about it! The very things that make winter more difficult and the set of demands and cautions for wintertime navigation so critical are similar and absolutely true for marriage in this season. While there are demands and cautions, there certainly are many joys and blessings associated with this season. It just takes extra caution and determination.

Be extra cautious and deliberate

Black ice is a treacherous thing. It looks like it is just a wet surface on the highway. Cars travel along at normal rates of speed as drivers believe they are driving on wet but safe highways. Without notice, unsuspecting drivers are suddenly on black ice. It is the most profoundly terrifying situation in which to find yourself. Your car spins wildly and often crashes out of control! Traffic warnings are often issued such as, "Allow yourself some extra time as you head out this morning. There are still icy spots, and you are going to need to exercise extra caution!"

The Apostle Paul warned the believers in Ephesus by writing, "See then that ye walk circumspectly, not as fools, but as wise" (Ephesians 5:15). The idea of "circumspectly" has to do with "walking accurately, diligently, or carefully." While this is important for every season of marriage, the wintertime season demands extra caution and carefulness of purpose.

Living circumspectly or carefully can be beautifully lived out in this wintertime season of marriage. There are several issues that are very typical in this season of marriage that require extra caution. Think of a few of these areas and talk with your spouse about these matters of life and marriage.

- *It is easy to become impatient.* Ask the Lord to help you to be careful with your spouse. Ask the Lord to help you to be long-suffering.

  Paul told Timothy, his beloved son in the faith, "I obtained mercy, that in me first Jesus Christ might show forth all long-suffering, for a pattern to them which should hereafter believe on Him to life everlasting" (1 Timothy 1:16).

  It was not easy for the Apostle Paul to be experiencing the extreme hardships of his life; however, he realized that in the hard time the Lord Jesus was ever present with him. This awesome Lord Jesus wanted to develop a long-suffering spirit in Paul's life that made it possible to extend mercy to others. The same can be true for you. Do you find yourself at times being impatient with your spouse or your circumstances? Ask God to help you to extend 'mercy,' which is the act of holding back what someone really may deserve.

- *It is easy to become fearful.* This season of life is marked by significant changes which sometimes occur quickly. While health-related issues and major adjustments can occur in the other seasons of marriage, they are typical and almost to be expected in this season of marriage.

Frankly, you and your spouse are growing older. Fear of the unknown circumstances of life is typical in this season. The good news is that if you and your spouse are believers, while you don't know what the immediate future holds, your Heavenly Father certainly does. He can be trusted in every circumstance of life.

Not all fear is wrong. There is a right kind of fear. The safest wintertime drivers are those who, because of healthy fear, drive cautiously. Likewise in your marriage, you and your spouse must have a healthy fear of your great God. Think of what the Bible tells you and your spouse.

"Now this is the commandment, and these are the statutes and judgments which the Lord your God has commanded to teach you, that you may observe them in the land which you are crossing over to possess, that you may fear the Lord your God, to keep all his statutes and his commandments which I commanded you, you and your son and your grandson, all the days of your life, and that your days may be prolonged " (Deuteronomy 6:1 NKJV).

The same counsel that Moses gave to the second generation of God's people in the wilderness is great for you and your spouse in this season of your life. A healthy reverence, respect, and actual terror at the Lord's awesome holiness provide a splendid testimony to your adult children and your grandchildren. This is the right kind of fear.

Unfortunately many who are your age live out their years gripped by the wrong kind of fear. Have you feared these things? Fear that your health or the health of someone you love will worsen? Fear that your spouse will die and you will be left without him or her? Fear that financially you will not have enough funds with which to retire? These and a dozen other fears can grip your heart and not only ruin your day, they can rob you of the joy that the Lord wants you to have and share.

This is a great place to stop for a moment. As you and your spouse read through this section, take a moment together to open God's Word and see what He has to say about fears. Talk with your spouse about these verses.

- Deuteronomy 3:21-22
- Isaiah 43:1
- Isaiah 43:5
- Luke 12:31-32
- 1 John 4:18

You might be thinking, "Yes, these verses are fine; however, I have really big problems that cause me fear."

So did King David. He wrote, "The Lord is my light and my salvation; whom shall I fear? The Lord is the strength of my life; of whom shall I be afraid? When the wicked, even my enemies and my foes, came upon me to eat up my flesh, they stumbled and fell. Though an host should encamp against me, my heart shall not fear: though war should rise against me, in this will I be confident. One thing have I desired of the Lord, that will I seek after; that I may dwell in the house of the Lord all the days of my life, to behold the beauty of the Lord, and to inquire in His temple. For in the time of trouble He shall hide me in His pavilion: in the secret of His tabernacle shall He hide me; He shall set me upon a rock. Wait on the Lord: be of good courage, and He shall strengthen thine heart: wait, I say, on the Lord" (Psalm 27:1-5, 14).

With the Lord's help, the application of His Word, fellowship with His people, and time alone with the Lord in prayer, there is great help for fear.

- ***It is easy to become grumpy and demanding.*** Being demanding and grumpy come readily in every season of life and marriage, but this season really lends itself to growing old and grumpy. You and your spouse may be dealing with situations that you would not choose for yourselves. You may have been very patient most of your life, now suddenly you find yourself getting mad over little things. Your patience is short and demands are great. These emotions range from mild annoyance to moderate aggravation to full-fledged anger.

There is help and hope available! What a great reminder the Apostle Paul provides for us as he writes concerning the fruit that the Holy Spirit wants to grow in the lives of you and your spouse. "But the fruit of the Spirit is love, joy, peace, long-suffering, gentleness, goodness, faith, meekness, temperance: against such there is no law" (Galatians 5:22-23).

The word "temperance" has the idea of self-control. In what ways do you and your spouse need to grow in the fruit of the Holy Spirit?

- ***It is easy to become a pew-sitter.***
  Don't pack up and retire from your local church.

  While you may not be able to keep up with the boys and girls in their game time at church, you are still very much needed. Paul reminded Titus to encourage the older men and women (Titus 2:2-5) to be useful, serving, and being an example to the younger. You still have much to offer.

What are you leaving for an inheritance?

"A good man leaves an inheritance to his children's children" (Proverbs 13:22).

The entire family gathered at Uncle Charlie's because he and Uncle Martin knew how Grandpa had prepared his will. It would be a great blessing for the entire family. Grandpa had loved the Lord and had lived a consistent Godly life. Now after his Homegoing, not only would the will impact Grandpa's children, it would be directed especially toward his grandchildren.

It was a lengthy will because Grandfather loved long conversations. The last few lines were especially powerful. He closed his will by stating, "The Bible says that a good man leaves an inheritance for his grandchildren. You can see that there are some finances but not a lot. The best thing that I can leave to you is that your Grandmother and I taught your parents the way of the Lord. They seem to be following the Lord at the time this is being written, but I am concerned about some of you grandchildren.

"If you are a Christian, your actions do not show that you are. Grandmother and I so want you to be with us in Heaven that I want to remind you that there is only one way for salvation, and that is through Christ (John 14:6), and it is by accepting His gift (Ephesians 2:8-9). I love each of you and will be looking forward to our grand reunion (1 Thessalonians 4:13-18)."

Uncle Charlie put the will down and had a tender but pointed conversation with the family. What an inheritance Grandfather had left. How about you? What are you leaving your children and grandchildren?

A Godly and gracious life consistently lived provides a wonderful blessing to all. As a grandparent you should be able to demonstrate the following things to your grandchildren.

- Concerning the Lord Jesus Christ, I learned to trust Him (Acts 16:31);
- Concerning the Bible, I learned to treasure it (Psalm 119:72, 127);
- Concerning sin, I learned to turn from it (Romans 6:22);
- Concerning my many blessings, I learned to thank the Lord for them (Psalm 110:4-5);
- Concerning my children, I learned to teach them (Deuteronomy 6:7).

Dealing with days of pain

One of the most difficult things about this season of life is learning how to deal with pain. As your body grows older, the minor little discomforts can grow into greater aches and pains. Wise believers learn to ask the Lord to keep them from resentment and pity parties when painful days come. There is great help for painful days.

The most difficult thing that you could ever face is not painful days for yourself. It would be the days of pain that your spouse may face. Let me share with you what I am learning in my chronic pain.

No one enjoys pain. No one enjoys hospitalization; however, even in the most difficult of days, don't allow anything to drive a wedge between you and your spouse. God has great blessings for your marriage. He has made awesome provision for you and your spouse, even when life is very difficult.

Talk about the ways the Lord desires to help you. Take time to look up the references and share with each other what your great God says about handling painful days.

- There is a special fellowship or sharing together with the Lord when life hurts (Philippians 3:10).
- There is an outworking of pain that results in a clearer focus on how short life is and how long eternity is (2 Corinthians 4:17).
- There is a quiet constant reminder that while you are weak, He is so strong (2 Corinthians 12:9-10). Learning more about His strength is such a blessing. Being reminded of weakness is not pleasant, but it is necessary.
- There is an assurance that you are not alone in times of pain. In fact, the pain you experience is not unique to you (1 Corinthians 10:13). As you proceed through this time, there will be plenty of people with whom you will be able to associate and share (2 Corinthians 1:3-4).
- There is a wonderful sense of security that no matter what the battle experience may be, the Lord really is the Rock that is higher than yourself (Psalm 61:1-2).
- There is the knowledge that this is not wasted time. There are lessons in the "He maketh me to lie down" times of my life. (Ask the Lord to help you learn them quickly, so you don't have to repeat a lot of these lessons.) He is the Lord of schedules, which includes the stops as well as the times of going (Psalm 27:14).
- There is great joy in knowing that wonderful day is coming closer and closer when the Lord Himself will dwell with us, He will wipe away all tears from our eyes and there will be no more pain (Revelation 21:1-4).

Help your spouse by getting your life in order

As stated earlier, this is not the season in which to become morbid. For you and your spouse to be the very best friends that you can possibly be is going to require that you determine to get your life in order and share important things clearly with your spouse

Think of Henry and Sam

"Well, I think such talk is foolish!" Henry said with a sharp tone in his voice. "Who wants to think such morbid thoughts," he continued as he looked at his friend across the table at the diner.

Sam was more than a little embarrassed. Henry was hard of hearing, so everything Henry said came out loudly. Out of the corner of his eye, Sam saw the folks at the next table turn and look at them. "They must be wondering what in the world I just said to Henry," he thought to himself. "Maybe I shouldn't press it," he continued thinking as he set his cup of coffee down.

"Pipe down, Henry," Sam said to his friend. "You don't have to let the whole diner know what I was talking about, you old goat!" Sam said grinning. "You still don't think you need hearing aids. And don't you argue with me; you still think Harry Truman is the president!" Sam kidded his friend.

The two men were glad when their breakfast arrived. After thanking the Lord for the food, Henry looked up at his friend and said, "Hey. Back to the 'getting your life in order' and lists and stuff. You okay? You aren't dying on me, are you?"

Wiping his mouth and placing the piece of toast on the plate, Sam fired back, "No, you old goat, I'm not dying. At least I don't think I am. But that's just the point. Remember when Harry died two months ago? Well, Karen visited Harry's wife this week. In fact, come to think of it, his death was more than two months ago, wasn't it?"

"Nearly four months," Henry grunted as he plowed into the eggs.

"That's the point. Like I said," Sam looked at his friend, "Karen visited Barbara this week. Karen comes home from the visit and tells me that Barbara and her two sons were trying to find and make sense of Harry's papers."

"Papers! What papers?" Henry asked. He continued working on those eggs.

"Important papers. Like—did he have a life insurance policy somewhere? Did he have mutual funds, and if so, where were they? Poor Barbara, she didn't even know if they had funds in any savings account!" Sam said. "When Karen came home telling me that, I decided right then and there that I needed to write her a note and let her know the important stuff and where they're located," Sam continued. "You can call me a hopeless romantic, but I really do love my Karen, and I would never want her to go through what Barb is facing. You ought to do the same thing for Shirley, you old goat!" Sam said, kicking him under the table.

"You always kick me under the table when you are trying to make a point, you old coot!" Henry growled. People from four different tables were now looking at them. "What are they looking at?" Henry asked. "So what are the things that I should put on my list of stuff?"

What a great talk the guys had that morning. It was disturbing to both men that poor Barbara didn't even know the basic things about their finances.

It would be many years later that the time came for Henry to go Home to be with the Lord. His death was very sudden and came as a shock to his family. Shirley's children rushed to the hospital and then went with their mom back to her home. As she hugged her children, the thought hit Shirley, "A note. Henry told me that if something happened to him that he had a note to me. Now where did he tell me it was located?" she wondered. "Bill and Nancy, several years ago your dad told me that if something happened, that there would be a note from him telling everything I needed to know. I've got to stop and think where he told me that note would be," Shirley said to her children.

"Mom, I know where the note is," Nancy said. "One day when we were all going out to supper, you were finishing getting ready, and Dad said to me, 'Nan, I don't want to get all mushy about stuff, but I wrote a note to your mom and you guys this week. Sam got me to thinking about stuff. When I die, it has everything she and you guys need to know. It's upstairs in the little drawer, inside the bigger dresser drawer.' I was crying when you came into the room. You asked if I was all right, and I pretended that it was probably just my hormones. Mom, it was Daddy. He told me that he loved you and wanted you to have it as easy as possible, if he died first."

Later that afternoon, Shirley wanted the family to be with her when she opened Henry's note. It was more of a letter than a note.

"Are you sure that you don't want to read it alone?" Bill asked. By now the other two children, Hunter and Marlene, together with their families, were with Shirley in her home. "We would perfectly understand if this is private and you don't want to share it with everyone," Marlene insisted.

Shirley opened the letter, and immediately overwhelmed with emotion, she needed help reading it. "Mom, would you like me to read it?" Hunter asked.

"I surely would," Shirley replied. Hunter took the letter, cleared his voice and read,

"Hello Shirley and the rest of my family. Now don't cry, any of you guys. First, let me say that you know that I am saved. I asked Jesus Christ to be my Savior when I was only six. I didn't live as good as I should of for a long time. I mean, I could've done better. Sorry I didn't. But I later did better when I decided to live for the Lord.

I'm not too good at writing. I'm really not too good at saying things. But secondly, let me say that I love each and every one of you. I am so thankful for the wonderful years of being married to you, Shirley. You are the best wife I could have ever had. Oh man, I gotta stop crying. But it's true Shirley. You are the best. I also love my children, and I couldn't be happier with the spouses they married. The best part of it all is that you guys gave us grandchildren. That maybe didn't sound good. But what I mean is that I surely love each of them.

Hunter, you probably are going to be the only one who can read this without crying. So I expect that unless your mother peeks at this ahead of time, you might be the one reading it."

Hunter stopped reading in order to wipe his eyes as he said, "Why in the world did Dad have to say that to me. I was doing pretty well until then." Within a moment or two he returned to Dad's note.

"Nan and Marlene have young ones to care for, so Bill and Hunter, I want you to help Mom with the important papers. Here's what I want you to know, my dear wife.

- *I don't know if Mom will remember the combination of the safe, so let me write it out. Turn two times to the right. Turn left and stop at 35. Turn right to 17. Turn left and stop at 3 on the second time around.*

Enjoying the Seasons

- *Inside you will find our wills. Our attorney's card with her address and phone number is paper-clipped on the outside. Not only did we update our wills, we have health care proxies and a living will. It's in there.*
- *I have a life insurance policy with Security Mutual. You will find the agent's name, address and telephone number on his business card right inside the packet.*
- *I have a portfolio of mutual funds with two different companies. Both of the companies and their financial guys and their information are in the yellow envelope that says PORTFOLIO on it.*
- *We have two different checking accounts. I know Mom uses the one checkbook all the time, but I am afraid that she will forget the second one. It is located inside my desk in my room upstairs. Look in the top right drawer. I keep it right behind the bank statements. Yes, Hunter, I still keep the written bank statements. Ha! Guess maybe you won't think it is funny right now. Sorry about that.*
- *The house is paid for, so that will be good.*
- *The titles to the car and truck are in the safe in the plastic baggie. I still owe on the truck but should have it paid in a year."*

Hunter smiled, looked up from the letter he held and said, "Oh Dad, you are something. Dad apparently got the letter out at a later time and wrote, "Nope. Forget the owing on the truck. Paid it off and will take Mom out to supper to celebrate.

- *Our birth certificates, social security information, marriage certificate, and my military discharge papers, if you need them for anything, are in the blue packet on the little shelf in the safe.*
- *Mom and Nan know what I want for funeral arrangements, and they will talk to everybody about that. Be sure to have folks sing lots and talk about me little.*
- *I've been getting retirement pension payments since I turned 66. Those papers are in my desk upstairs. I didn't keep them in the safe because I have to talk to those people too much. Now you boys will have to talk to those folks. Sorry for you!*
- *Our tax papers are in the filing cabinet in the garage. I have them filed under the G. Want to know why? It's G for GRUMBLE, which is what I do every time I file our taxes."*

The emotions of Hank's family were so ragged at this point that the immediate reaction of bursting into laughter soon turned back into tears. "Dad, you are such a hoot," Marlene managed to say. Hunter returned the family to the letter as he read,

- *"The passwords that are important are in the small white envelope inside the safe. I don't like internet stuff, but there are some passwords that I wrote out.*
- *I have a credit card with our local bank in addition to the card credit Mom and I use. This card is for my little Ebay business. It's in my wallet. So is my license and other stuff that I can't remember right now.*

I think this is all of our important papers. I'm glad that my Saturday morning breakfast friend Sam got me to thinking. I want to make this as easy for you, my dear Shirley and family, as I can. I love you all. To my grandchildren, I want you to know that your parents and grandma and I have all asked the Lord to be our Savior. I know that Liz, Tammy, Derek, Peter, Lanny, and Danny have all been saved. If there's any to come after that, you need to be saved too. I will be waiting in Heaven for you.

Love,

Henry, Dad, and Grandpa

PS Now stop that crying 'cause I'm having a great time!"

Henry would be missed by his family and many friends. How much it meant to Shirley and her family that Henry had written such a letter! It shared his love, his heart, and the important information that his family would need.

How about you? Your family truly will be greatly helped if you would write such a letter. At least make a list of where you have placed the important papers that your survivors will need to locate. Get your house in order and make out a list!

Think about these questions

1. Have you and your spouse talked about your important papers and where they are located?

2. Have you and your spouse prepared a will?

3. Do you have a health care proxy and have you declared your intentions concerning a living will?

4. Have you written a note to your spouse and family that will be a living legacy for them to treasure in the years ahead?

The joy and anticipation of meeting the Lord

What a great time for you and your spouse to look forward to meeting the Lord Jesus Christ as you enjoy every day that the Lord gives you together. The Apostle John put it like this as he wrote, "Beloved, now are we the sons of God, and it does not yet appear what we shall be: but we know that, when He shall appear, we shall be like him: for we shall see Him as He is. And every man that hath this hope in him purifieth himself, even as he is pure" (1 John 3:2-3).

Be sure your spouse knows of your love. Live each day in such a way that there will be no regrets. Enjoy this season with your sweetheart. Ask the Lord to help you to grow older with graciousness. Reflect the goodness of your great God in your daily life.

Think about these questions

1. Which season would best describe your marriage?

2. What are the top five blessings that you are experiencing in this season of your marriage?

3. What are two or three of the most difficult things you are facing in this season of your marriage?

4. Take time to talk with your spouse about this. What are several things that you could determine to do to make this season of your marriage more enjoyable?

5. Have you and your spouse prepared your will? Do your spouse and children know where the important papers are located? Use Henry's letter as at least a guide.

6. Are you and your spouse best friends? If not, why not?

Now nineteen years later, Tim and Kirsten are still best friends. That little note from Grandpa Mitchell holds great value to both. Not only did it come from a dearly beloved grandfather, it held the key to their very successful marriage. They overcame every obstacle and are so glad they did.

You May Be Wondering

Are the people real? and what about the construction business? The people and business actually are real. Their names have been changed, but Tim and Kirsten, Ken and Alisha, as well as Uncle Hank, are the combination of multiple characters whom I have known and loved over the years. Mitchell and Sons Construction also had a name change, but the principles that were written by "Grandpa Mitchell" are the same principles that several very special builders have expressed to me over the years. Tragically the Madisons are real as well. While the characters and building company are renamed, please understand that the principles are real and the Word of God can be trusted and implemented.

Yes, "Tim and Kirsten" became and stayed best friends indeed.

You and your spouse can as well.

It is my prayer that there will be a little "dust" which is the evidence that you are working in this area in your marriage. Constructing a beautiful marriage is a lot like constructing a beautiful house!

Epilogue
So Now It Is Up To You!

What a Joy to be Married to your Best Friend!

Staying best friends when the honeymoon's over is not just the goal of this book. It is the will of your precious Lord as the Designer of marriage. Malachi provides a precious reminder that your spouse is your companion because of the covenant into which you have entered. A companion provides sweet encouragement, fellowship, and enjoyment on the journey of a lifetime.

For your spouse to become your best friend, you may have to do some marriage construction and make a little dust as you work! Let there be evidence that you and your spouse are working on your marriage.

Your view of God's Word

God's Word presents very strong directives and very practical principles to help you on this journey. Take God's Word seriously. Apply it personally. Think of what the psalmist wrote, "With my whole heart have I sought thee: let me not wander from Thy commandments. Thy word have I hid in mine heart, that I might not sin against Thee (Psalm 119:10-11).

The Apostle James provides great direction when he writes, "But be ye doers of the word, and not hearers only, deceiving your own selves. For if any be a hearer of the word, and not a doer, he is like a man beholding his natural face in a glass: for he beholds himself, and goes his way, and straightway forgets what manner of man he was" (James 1:22-24).

For those who hear God's Word but refuse to do it, James likens them to the person who looks in the mirror and sees a smudge on his face. He looks closely at the smudge and then turns and walks away, knowingly leaving the smudge on his face. This is not very wise, is it?

After placing your trust in the Lord to be your Savior, believe God's Word and do it. Love His Word to be wise. Practice God's Word to be holy.

How you view your marriage

Enjoy each day that the Lord gives you. Determine with your spouse that by His grace you will view your marriage in much the same way Grandpa Mitchell encouraged his grandson, Tim. Grandpa was so right. Tim and Kirsten were encouraged to build their marriage by adopting the same principles by which he built beautiful houses. They listened and were glad they did. You will be, too!

In conclusion, think of the awesome statement our Savior made the night before He went to the cross for our sins. He told His disciples, "If ye know these things, happy are ye if you do them" (John 13:17). Often the problem is not that couples do not know what to do. Often the problem lies in the fact that couples are not willing to do what they know they should be doing.

Be wise. Do what you know the Lord wants you to do. Don't be stubborn. Don't try to change your spouse. Ask the Lord to bring about the changes in both of your lives that only He is able to do.

It is my prayer that there will be a little "dust" which is the evidence that you are working in this area in your marriage. Constructing a beautiful marriage is a lot like constructing a beautiful house!

Check out these other resources by Dr. Michael Peck

- *Steps of Joy—Preparing for Membership in My Local Church*
  available at www.bcpusa.org

These are available at Regular Baptist Press, Schaumburg, Illinois. Find them at www.rbpstore.org.

- *From This Day Forward—*
  Preparing Couples for the Journey of a Lifetime

- *Connecting—Developing Closeness on the Journey of a Lifetime*

Visit www.michaelpeck.org for media as well as publication resources. Subscribe to "Dr. Mike's Daily Prescription" on the homepage of his website.

www.ingramcontent.com/pod-product-compliance
Lightning Source LLC
LaVergne TN
LVHW051051080426
835508LV00019B/1820